Clement Haynsworth,
the Senate,
and the Supreme Court

Clement Haynsworth, the Senate, and the Supreme Court

John P. Frank

University Press of Virginia

CHARLOTTESVILLE AND LONDON

THE UNIVERSITY PRESS OF VIRGINIA
Copyright © 1991 by the Rector and Visitors
of the University of Virginia

First published 1991

Frontispiece: Courtesy of Mrs. Clement F. Haynsworth, Jr.

Library of Congress Cataloging-in-Publication Data
Frank, John Paul, 1917–
    Clement Haynsworth, the Senate, and the Supreme Court / John P.
Frank.
        p.   cm.
    Includes bibliographical references and index.
    ISBN 0-8139-1291-1
    1. United States. Supreme Court—Officials and employees—
Selection and appointment.   2. Judges—United States—Selection and
appointment.   3. Political questions and judicial power—United
States.   4. Haynsworth, Clement F. (Clement Furman), 1912–
I. Title.
    KF8742.F7   1991
    347.73'2634—dc20
    [347.3073534]   90-40349
                                                                          CIP

Printed in the United States of America

Contents

My Partners at Lewis and Roca and I
Dedicate Any Royalties from This Work to
the University of Virginia Graduate Program for Judges
with Respect for Its Program to Improve the
Quality of Appellate Justice in America

Foreword

This is a book by a gifted writer about the nomination of Judge Clement F. Haynsworth, Jr., to the United States Supreme Court and the Senate's defeat of that nomination. Judge Haynsworth was one of the truly great federal judges. I am happy to have this opportunity to pay tribute to him.

My friendship with Judge Haynsworth—whom I think of simply as "Clement"—dates back to the early 1950s. He was appointed by President Eisenhower in 1957 to the United States Court of Appeals for the Fourth Circuit, which was headquartered in my home city of Richmond. His appointment was widely approved by the bar, as his qualifications for the federal bench were the highest.

A native of Greenville, South Carolina, Haynsworth graduated summa cum laude from Furman University and then from the Harvard Law School in 1936. His family roots in South Carolina date back to long before the Revolution. Indeed, Furman University was founded by his great-great-grandfather. He practiced in Greenville in his family law firm of Haynsworth and Haynsworth and served in the navy during World War II. His obituary in the *Washington Post* of November 23, 1989, correctly stated that Haynsworth "brought to the bench a reputation as a top-flight lawyer . . . [whose] judicial opinions were known for the workmanlike way in which they were crafted."

This book describes the changes in the membership of the Supreme Court from 1968 to 1970. President Nixon, in campaign speeches, had promised to nominate a southerner for any vacancy that occurred on the Court. When Justice Fortas resigned, the president nominated Clement Haynsworth. I strongly supported him and was successful in obtaining support for the nomination from all but one of the past presidents of the American Bar Association. Despite wide support for Haynsworth from the bar and from leaders in the South, the Senate by a vote of fifty-five to forty-five rejected the nomination.

I repeat what I have said before: The defeat of this eminently qualified jurist was "purely political" and reflected adversely on the Senate rather than on Clement Haynsworth. He accepted his defeat with grace and without bitterness. Perhaps it is not generally known that Haynsworth considered retiring from the fourth circuit court of appeals. I joined with others in urging him not to do this. Happily he remained, and despite serious health problems he continued to sit until a few months before his death on November 22, 1989.

As may be evident from what I have said, in my view Clement Haynsworth was an exceptionally able—indeed a distinguished—federal judge. As John P. Frank, the author of this book, emphasizes, Haynsworth also was "a perfect gentleman," a loyal friend, and as fine a human being as I have ever known.

After Haynsworth was not confirmed, the president nominated G. Harrold Carswell, an undistinguished federal judge from Florida. References frequently were made in the press and elsewhere to "the Haynsworth and Carswell nominations" despite the fact that two more dissimilar judges would not be easy to find. Yet, this mindless misjoinder of names occasionally is made even today.

I was a member of the bar of the fourth judicial circuit from the early 1950s. I observed with admiration Haynsworth's leadership of the circuit after he became chief judge in 1964. Its annual conferences were held in late June alternatively at the Homestead and the Greenbrier. These are two famous "old-world" resorts that provide an elegant setting for serious work as well as for social and athletic activities.

Haynsworth had a slight stutter in his speaking voice, but this never deterred him from presiding over a meeting with great skill or from speaking with force on any subject. After conference meetings on Thursday and Friday, there would be a Saturday morning session at which prominent professors—such as Charles Alan Wright from the University of Texas— would conduct a program on Supreme Court decisions during the term just ending. The conference adjourned at lunch on Saturday. For many years my wife Jo and I would remain in the hotel overnight for the purpose of having dinner Saturday evening with the Haynsworths in their suite. Professor and Mrs. Wright, perhaps another couple or two, also would dine that evening with the Haynsworths. As would be true only in the South, and possibly in the mid-twentieth century only in South Carolina, Judge Haynsworth always referred to his lovely and gracious wife as "Miss Dorothy."

America lost the services of a potentially great Supreme Court justice when the Senate defeated Judge Haynsworth's nomination. But America's loss was the fourth circuit's gain. Judge Haynsworth is destined to be remembered by many simply for the events recounted in this book. Certainly, his nomination and defeat were significant events in American history. For me, at least, he left a much more significant mark on American law through his scholarly and distinguished opinions as a fourth circuit judge. Indeed, I believe it was the quality of his work on the fourth circuit after his defeat that has led many to recognize the injustice of the Senate's 1969 vote.

LEWIS F. POWELL, JR.

Preface

This book deals with the 1969–70 events of the resignation of Justice Abe Fortas from the Supreme Court, the defeated nominations to replace him of judges Clement F. Haynsworth, Jr., and G. Harrold Carswell, and the nomination and confirmation of Judge Harry Blackmun. Because my own identification with some of these subjects and persons and events must inevitably affect the history I recount, a reader is entitled to know where the possible biases are. I began serious work on the study of Supreme Court appointments under the guidance of the great American historian Charles Beard in 1939. This resulted in a published account of the appointments up to 1941 in the *Wisconsin Law Review* of that year. I also happen to have been heavily involved in development of the law of disqualification of judges, a topic which occupies many pages in this volume. Disqualification is the law governing when a judge may or may not participate in a particular case. That work began with a publication in the *Yale Law Journal* in 1947 which, as it happened, was at the root of a good deal of the Senate discussion in 1969.

So much for subject matter. I knew Justice Abe Fortas extremely well. I was personal assistant to Secretary of the Interior Harold Ickes and to Under Secretary Fortas in 1943–44; I practiced law on occasion in the Fortas office after he went into private practice; we were together on some important matters, and we were genuine friends. I assisted him in preparing some of his testimony when he was nominated for the chief justiceship in 1968. I was not involved in any way in the events that led to his resignation, but it is my unequivocal view, based on a twenty-five-year friendship, that he was a man of perfect integrity. There was poor judgment on occasion as this book will narrate, but Fortas was an honorable man.

When Judge Haynsworth was nominated to the Supreme Court, I knew him but not well. I was called upon by the Senate Judiciary Committee to appear as a witness at the Haynsworth hearings because of my work in the field of disqualification. What was a casual acquaintance then became a major friendship of a lifetime. I regard Judge Haynsworth as quite possibly the most perfect gentleman I have ever known. He was an absolutely honorable man; unlike Fortas, not even his judgment could be faulted. I regard as one of the great privileges of my life that I should have been allowed, with Justice Lewis F. Powell, Jr., of the Supreme Court, to make dedicatory remarks for the Clement F. Haynsworth, Jr., Federal Building in Greenville, South Carolina, an extraordinary but unanimous apology in stone from the Congress of the United States for having traduced the character of a good man.

In the nomination of Judge Carswell, my personal role was minor; I opposed him publicly and was one of the signers of a statement organized by Judge Samuel Rosenman and others which was widely publicized in opposition. I have never met Judge Carswell and have no basis for a personal opinion as to his character; professionally I thought him far below the standard required for the Supreme Court. Justice Blackmun I did not know at all when he was appointed, and we have only the most casual acquaintance at the present time. I have come to esteem him professionally very highly, but this has no personal influence on any judgment involved here.

Perhaps some neutrality works its way into this account because my normal personal and political affiliation was with senators Birch Bayh, Edward Kennedy, and Joseph Tydings, three of the Haynsworth-Carswell opponents. Had I been elected president in 1968 which, alas, I was not, I would have made none of these appointments, and had I been attorney general in 1969, equally improbable, I would not have participated in forcing Justice Fortas off the Court. Perhaps one can achieve some objectivity through earnest regret at the series of events.

On the Fortas portion of the story, I have my own files, and I have been given whatever assistance Mrs. Fortas and the justice's good friend Clark Clifford could give me; this was in fact not much. Kenneth Pringle, a Washington attorney, helped me with those materials. In 1971 Judge Haynsworth dictated for me a comprehensive oral history of his impressions of the confirmation proceedings, a memorandum which, since he is now dead, I am free to use under our original agreement, and I do use it here. Professor Charles Alan Wright of the University of Texas Law School was an active player on the Haynsworth team and has shared his papers as well as a memoir; he has also given me editorial counsel beyond the call of friendship.

My able assistant, Sarah Shew, gathered and organized the voluminous Haynsworth papers, now in the Furman University library at Greenville and generously shared by that institution, and additionally gathered papers in Washington and did the entire organizational job of the documents used in this volume. This includes considerable information obtained under the Freedom of Information Act from the Department of Justice and all files of the Senate Judiciary Committee, which the then chairman of that committee, Senator Strom Thurmond of South Carolina, courteously made available.

In addition, the then assistant attorney general, Johnnie Mac Walters, who was very much in the thick of the Haynsworth affair and was active in the Carswell and Blackmun appointments, has shared his papers with me and counseled me generously. As an immensely reliable editor, he has checked the manuscript not once but twice. The then attorney general, John Mitchell, involved in all four of these events, shared his recollections in a friendly and gracious interview. The leading civil rights opponent of Haynsworth and Carswell, Joseph L. Rauh of Washington, D.C., shared his files, no longer very voluminous. The main untapped source remains the personal papers of Senator Birch Bayh of Indiana, the leader in the defeats of both Haynsworth and Carswell. They have been given to Indiana University at Bloomington but have never been organized for effective use. My own papers as to all four of these appointments, apart from the voluminous printed hearings and congressional debates, stand cheek by jowl some four linear feet. The law clerks at Lewis and Roca, the firm with which I practice in Phoenix, Arizona, gave much time to analyzing these materials; I am especially obligated to Suanne Rudley and Suzanne Murphy. My wife, Lorraine W. Frank, has helped as a valued editor.

As to Judge Carswell, I am dependent on published sources and the papers produced under the Freedom of Information Act, and I have some similar sources as to Justice Blackmun.

Four books are very helpful. In 1972 Robert Shogan published *A Question of Judgment* (Indianapolis: Bobbs Merrill Company, 1972), a book on the Fortas appointment. Shogan was a highly experienced *News-week* reporter. The first two-thirds of the book is a limited Fortas biography setting the stage for his appointment as chief justice and later for his withdrawal from the Court. The chief justice controversy is vividly described. The last third is on his resignation.

Unfortunately for Shogan's book, Chief Justice Warren declined to meet with him or discuss the subject, believing that the matter was best left at rest. The Warren papers have since been released, are used in this volume, and permit an understanding which was not available to Shogan. A later work, Professor Bruce Murphy's *Fortas: The Rise and Ruin of a Supreme Court Justice* (New York: W. Morrow, 1988), did make use of the Warren papers and hence tells a further story. So does Laura Kalman's *Abe Fortas* (New Haven: Yale Univ. Press, 1990), pp. 317–78, on the chief justiceship and the resignation.

The book *Decision* by Richard Harris (New York: E. P. Dutton and Company, Inc., 1971), on the Carswell nomination, is comprehensive. Harris first published his book as a series of articles in the *New Yorker*.

My own materials supplement the published sources as to Fortas, Carswell, and Blackmun. The statement of Judge Haynsworth is wholly unused elsewhere, and the Haynsworth, Walters, and other files have not been used in any previous publication.

Clement Haynsworth,
the Senate,
and the Supreme Court

Introduction

On May 14, 1969, Supreme Court Justice Abe Fortas resigned. On May 12, 1970, the Senate confirmed Justice Harry Blackmun to take his place. President Nixon's first two choices for the vacancy, Judge Clement F. Haynsworth, Jr., of Greenville, South Carolina, and Judge G. Harrold Carswell of Tallahassee, Florida, were nominated and defeated in the interim.

These four events make a unique chapter in the history of the Supreme Court. The cluster resulted not only in filling a vacancy but in contributing to the rewriting of federal statutes on judicial administration and the revision of the code of ethics for judges. Most important of all, the series bred great introspection on qualities to be expected of a Supreme Court justice and the role of the United States Senate in considering a presidential nomination. It is the story of those events that is told here.

Because there is substantial writing on the Fortas resignation and the Carswell nomination, and because there is very little to be said about the Blackmun nomination, I have included just enough as to those episodes to put the Haynsworth experience in context. At the same time, all four are clearly connected. Without the Fortas resignation there would have been no vacancy to fill; but, more important for the sequence of events, without the hostilities engendered by the Fortas experience, there would have been less counterhostility toward Haynsworth and Carswell; and without the exhaustion caused by all three, the Blackmun appointment might not have glided through so easily. One does not need to know all about the Fortas and the Carswell incidents to understand the Haynsworth story, but I do include enough of each of the other events to make a coherent sequence.

In the historical sense, this is essentially a book on the nomination and defeat of Judge Haynsworth to the Supreme Court. In the political science sense, it is a case study on method, on the means by which a Supreme Court nomination may be combated. Because the Carswell episode provides a rich study of confirmation methodology, I have included the phases of the Carswell matter that particularly illustrate the tactics of confirmation controversy.

As will be developed in the pages following, much but not all of the opposition to Judge Haynsworth was makeweight. In the history of Supreme Court appointments and the resistance to them, it is almost a rule that a makeweight is a more effective political tool than a policy reason. Where a Supreme Court appointment is resisted seriously, and most of them are not, the real reason usually will be discontent with the opinions it is anticipated the appointee will express. This is normally not regarded as a good reason, likely to succeed, for opposing an appointment. While there have been oppositions on the merits, as when the appointment of Chief Justice Hughes was opposed in 1931 by those who thought he had become a "tool of the interests," or Judge John J. Parker, also in 1931, on the grounds that he was allegedly antilabor, a more normal device is for the opponents to find something on which they can hang their hats which may well be tangential to the appointment.

For significant illustrations, Justice Brandeis was opposed in 1916 in the longest and most strenuous confirmation battle of all. The resistance was, in fact, based on the anticipated liberalism of the Brandeis decisions, but the opposition verbalized its position in terms of extremely flimsy criticisms of the Brandeis ethics at the bar. In the case of Justice Harlan Stone, the true opposition was the objection by Senator Burton K. Wheeler of Montana to Stone's handling, as attorney general, of a matter adverse to Wheeler's client; the nature of the opposition again became ethical with objections to Stone's law firm's handling of a particular matter in the Delaware courts. When Justice Felix Frankfurter was nominated, the opponents who were concerned with his anticipated liberalism sought to paint him as a Communist. In the recent appointment of Justice William Rehnquist as chief justice, the real opposition was that he is the most conservative justice to sit on the Court in the past fifty years and combines with his point of view the skill to make that point of view extremely effective. The stated grounds involved Rehnquist's asserted role in a very minor election day fracas, and a second ground was an argument over whether he should have disqualified himself as a judge in a particular case because of some previous connection with the matter in the Department of Justice. The Congress had, in fact, expressly approved the rule of disqualification law that Justice Rehnquist had applied, but the furor was considerable all the same.

This is not to minimize the force of the opposition or its sincere purposiveness in any of the illustrative cases given. It is simply to say that the rules of the game of Supreme Court appointments may require the players to wear masks if they are going to participate.

The controversies of 1969–70 foreshadowed the controversy in 1987 over the nomination of Judge Robert H. Bork by President Reagan to the Supreme Court vacancy created by the resignation of Justice Lewis F. Powell, Jr., who, coincidentally, fills so large a role in this volume. This volume, which was essentially complete before the Bork nomination (which I opposed before the Senate Judiciary Committee), does not deal with that appointment; but the senatorial thinking about the proper role of the Senate in relation to Supreme Court nominations discussed here represents a stage in the development of that thinking which moved toward full application in the discussion of the senatorial role in Judge Bork's case.

This is a work without a hero. No Saint George slew all the dragons. It is not the noblest chapter in Supreme Court history. But we may learn from it.

I

The Fortas Vacancy

On May 14, 1969, Justice Abe Fortas resigned from the United States Supreme Court. The event was spectacular; it is the only time in history a justice has resigned under pressure from the press and the executive branch of the government.

The story is short and colorful. Fortas, a Tennessean by birth, had an extraordinary legal career. Editor in chief of the *Yale Law Journal*, he rapidly moved through the Washington chairs in the New Deal and World War II days with the Agricultural Adjustment Administration and the Securities and Exchange Commission (SEC) and then became general counsel for the Public Works Administration. From 1942 to 1946 he was under secretary of the Department of Interior and a significant adviser in San Francisco and London to the United States delegation to the United Nations during its formative period.

After the war Fortas joined his old friend Thurman Arnold in founding and developing a law firm later known as Arnold, Fortas and Porter and now as Arnold and Porter. The firm rapidly became a major presence in Washington, renowned not merely for its important business clients and litigation but for its role in the protection of civil liberties. During the period of the 1950s when Senator Joseph McCarthy of Wisconsin rode high, Arnold and Fortas undertook the defense of many of those pilloried, either in administrative agencies or by congressional committees. The most famous of these was the case of Owen Lattimore, where the firm, with Fortas heavily involved personally, won a total victory over the McCarthy charges. Perhaps his best-known nonpolitical but public litigation was a case establishing a widely used test for insanity in criminal cases and the case broadly establishing the right to counsel in criminal matters.[1]

Fortas's most famous client was Senator and later President Lyndon B. Johnson. Fortas handled for Johnson the very close vote matter by which Johnson obtained his initial Senate seat and was his regular counselor thereafter on personal and public matters. In 1965 Johnson, over considerable resistance from Fortas who truly did not want the job, appointed Fortas to the Supreme Court.[2]

In late spring 1968 Johnson again nominated Fortas, this time to be chief justice in place of Earl Warren, who was retiring. The Republicans, scenting victory in the fall which would enable them to appoint the next chief justice, engaged in vigorous resistance, including strenuous committee hearings. The resistance circled around two matters: first, on the role of Fortas as a justice who had continued to be an adviser from time to time to President Johnson on important policy matters; and second, on outside income the justice had received during his judicial tenure.

The role of Fortas as counselor to the president was not unusual. While some justices are appointed to the Court by presidents who do not know them, it is by no means remarkable that a president will be making a very personal appointment when he chooses a Supreme Court justice and that he will know the person very well. If the president is accustomed to relying upon his appointee for general matters of judgment before the appointment, his reliance may continue afterward. The practice will wither away as time introduces new presidents who may have no relations with the justice at all; but in the early period of the justice's term, such consultations are not infrequent. Thus, Justice Brandeis was a frequent adviser of President Wilson during World War I, and Chief Justice Taft was so occupied as an adviser to presidents Harding, Coolidge, and Hoover that his biographer includes a chapter titled "Presidential Adviser" in his biography of that chief justice. Justice, later Chief Justice, Stone was a frequent adviser of President Hoover, as well as his fellow exerciser in what was called the Medicine Ball Cabinet.[3] There are many other illustrations.

A further objection much pressed to Fortas was that he had accepted a $15,000 fee for a series of lectures at American University. This sum had been raised by his former law partner Paul Porter from five wealthy contributors to the university, and the argument was advanced that the receipt of this money, raised by that means, was corrupting. The amount is sufficiently high, as compared with traditional university salaries, that it has been more fairly criticized as insensitivity to probable attack.

The Judiciary Committee held hearings on these various matters which filled some 1,400 pages and lasted from July 11 to 23, 1968, and then, on the American University matter, were picked up again on September 13 and 16. The report of the Judiciary Committee was favorable, the committee finding no objections to relations between a president and a justice so long as those relations did not "touch upon judicial matters or affect the duties of the Supreme Court,"[4] and Fortas's relations did not; President Johnson's worries in this period were principally about the Vietnam War, and these were the principal matters of consultation.

But there were strong dissents, and the various objections had filled the summer and stretched into the fall so that with an unbreakable filibuster, the appointment could not be successfully considered by the Senate. At his own request, the name of Justice Fortas was withdrawn, and in consequence, succeeding president, Richard Nixon, was able to name Warren Burger to the chief justiceship. This politicization of the Fortas nomination by the Republicans undoubtedly contributed to a willingness by the Democrats to politicize the Haynsworth nomination a little later.

Justice Fortas came out of the 1968 defeat scarred but not badly wounded. There had been enormous professional support, and the dissenters were entirely those who disagreed with his opinions, as well as his conduct; the defeat was one of strategy and time. It was widely believed that Justice Black had advised Justice Fortas not to accept the chief justiceship because the opposition could stall his confirmation in the Senate, and if in fact that advice was given, it certainly proved sound. At the end of 1968 Fortas and his friends could take some small comfort from the enemies he had made.

The next year, 1969, was a different story. Before 1965, when Fortas was appointed to the Supreme Court, his firm had represented the interests of Louis E. Wolfson, who was also a friend of Fortas. These interests included two major companies, the New York Shipbuilding Corporation and Merritt-Chapman and Scott Corporation, a major heavy construction company. Wolfson sponsored the Wolfson Family Foundation, dedicated to the improvement of community relations and racial and religious cooperation. When Justice Arthur Goldberg resigned in 1965, there was immediately talk of the possibility of Fortas as his successor. Wolfson wrote

Fortas urging him to accept the position. However, Wolfson recognized the drain that the cut in salary would cause in Fortas's standard of living (there are no exact figures available, but Fortas must have made between five and ten times as much in the law practice as he would be paid as a Supreme Court justice) and suggested that Fortas might be associated with the Wolfson Foundation by way of useful service and income supplement.

Fortas and Wolfson discussed possible association with the foundation again shortly after the nomination. Fortas included the Wolfsons at a reception in his honor at the Court in October 1965, and shortly thereafter he arranged to become a consultant to the foundation for the figure of $20,000 a year for the rest of his life, a similar amount to be paid to his wife after his own death.[5] The foundation at the time was extremely modest but clearly had a capacity for great growth. Also at the time, Wolfson was under SEC investigation, which appeared to Fortas to be "purely technical" and of no great consequence. In January 1966 Fortas received his first—and last check—for $20,000.[6]

Wolfson was a major businessman—during this same period he also had a controlling interest in the District of Columbia Transit System—but he was not a model of corporate virtue. When some of his companies hit evil times, he dumped a good deal of stock in them, leaving the loss to be absorbed by the public, without compliance with certain SEC regulations. An SEC and later Justice Department investigation began. A Wolfson subordinate, Alex Rittmaster, informed the government and also did some name-dropping about Wolfson's prominent friend, Justice Fortas. A very close associate of Wolfson, Buddy Gerbert of Florida, was also said to have made many references to Justice Fortas. The only practical consequence of any impression of influence in the offing was for the United States attorney in New York, Robert Morgenthau, to make sure that the case was pushed even harder.[7]

In June 1966, six months after going on the foundation board and after receiving his first compensation, Fortas canceled his agreement with the foundation, agreeing only to finish the 1966 work. In the summer of 1966 Wolfson was, in fact, indicted by the Department of Justice in connection with certain stock transactions, and in December of that year Fortas returned to the foundation the $20,000 he had received. Thus, by the end of 1966 he had been in and out of the foundation, had performed some services, had received compensation, and had returned it.

These events were known in 1966 only to the foundation and to

Fortas. Although he had attended one foundation meeting at Jacksonville, Florida, there had then been no news story or other attention about his involvement. The SEC had referred the Wolfson investigation to the Department of Justice shortly before the Florida meeting; Fortas was in Florida on June 14–16 and resigned from the foundation upon his return to Washington on June 21.

In January 1967, according to Wolfson, he and Fortas met at the Deauville Hotel in Miami Beach. According to Wolfson, Fortas heard him out sympathetically but "made no offer of assistance"; there were no later meetings between the two.[8] In November 1967, in the first case against Wolfson, he was sentenced to a year in prison and fined $100,000. In a second prosecution, he was given eighteen additional months. The first conviction was sustained on appeal, and the second was reversed.[9]

The next two years, 1967 and 1968, went placidly by, but the Fortas roof fell in with a *Life* magazine article on May 4, 1969. The magazine began its investigation in 1968. The *Life* reporter related the Wolfson matter to United States Attorney Morgenthau, who immediately passed it on to then Attorney General Ramsey Clark. On Saturday, November 9, 1968, Clark met with Fortas and was satisfied that there was nothing consequential about the matter. When the matter came before Attorney General John N. Mitchell the next spring, he asked his legal adviser, William Rehnquist, as to a proper course of action. Rehnquist reported that if Fortas had, in fact, taken money to assist Wolfson, such conduct would be a crime and should be prosecuted.[10]

On April 1, 1969, the Supreme Court had declined to review Wolfson's conviction, thus ending the Wolfson matter so far as the Supreme Court was concerned; Justice Fortas had not participated in the decision. The *Life* story reported that Fortas was paid by the foundation "ostensibly" to assist in its good works projects, but that his "name was being dropped in strategic places by Wolfson and Gerbert in their effort to stay out of prison on the securities charge." The story asserted that Fortas's "extra judicial activity" with President Johnson "finally got him in trouble and cost him the job of Chief Justice" and that the American University fee was a "climax" for the opposition. The *Life* story offered no evidence, nor was any ever developed anywhere, that Fortas actually had intervened at any point in behalf of Wolfson; but it did cite two canons of ethics, one on the appearance of impropriety and the other on accepting "inconsistent duties."

The Florida meeting of the foundation on June 14, 1966, took place after the SEC had forwarded its complaints about Wolfson to the Justice Department, and a Wolfson associate later said that the SEC matter had been discussed with Fortas later at Ocala. In 1966 the foundation was a very small enterprise, and the $20,000 paid to Fortas was very nearly 20 percent of its income; Fortas's understanding was that he was going into the project to plan its expansion.

Before publishing its article, *Life* had asked Fortas if he cared to make a statement concerning his association with Wolfson. Fortas sent a letter to *Life*, printed in the story, which covered the preappointment business associations, mentioned the foundation, noted that he was present at the Florida meeting of the foundation, but did not discuss his financial arrangement. He expressly stated that he had not discussed Wolfson's business or legal affairs then or ever and said, "In fact, my recollection is that Mr. Wolfson himself was not present at the meeting of the Family Foundation." [11]

On May 4, immediately after the *Life* story, Fortas issued a 300-word statement on the matter. The *Life* story had not said that the Wolfson contract provided for a $20,000-a-year payment to Fortas for life and a similar payment thereafter to his wife, and Fortas did not mention that provision. His statement said that "the Wolfson family foundation tendered a fee to me. Concluding that I could not undertake the assignment, I returned the fee with my thanks." He had never performed any legal services for Wolfson after he came to the Supreme Court. The twelve-month gap between the "tender" and the "return" was not mentioned, nor were the contract and its terms. This failure to make prompt and full disclosure was the largest misfortune of the Fortas affair because the details quickly emerged and the failure to disclose them looked like a cover-up. The statement, in short, was a major tactical blunder. [12]

The *Life* story created a fire storm. The pressures demanding Fortas's resignation built at an amazing speed. Within a few days of the *Life* magazine article, some of Fortas's former supporters in his bid for chief justice of the Supreme Court suggested that he should resign from the Supreme Court. Many were concerned with the possibility that Fortas, in fact, had accepted a fee for legal services from Wolfson. Others were more concerned with the appearance of impropriety and the effect that it would have on the judiciary and on the Supreme Court. Most commentators insisted, at a minimum, that Fortas give a detailed explanation of his relationship with Wolfson. [13]

On May 7, 1969, Attorney General Mitchell called on Chief Justice

Warren to discuss the Fortas-Wolfson relationship. Mitchell carried with him what he described in a 1987 interview as a "packet of papers" which he left with the chief justice.[14] That packet consisted of five documents, each of which has been synopsized here. The first four were the papers making the arrangement for Fortas to serve as adviser to the foundation. The fifth was a letter from Fortas to the foundation of December 15, 1966, returning the compensation he had received. These papers confirmed the *Life* story to the extent that they established what it had asserted.

Any conversation between Warren and Mitchell was brief. As of 1987, Mitchell did not care to reveal its contents. However, he did tell the chief justice that more papers would be coming from the Justice Department, and on May 12, 1969, at 6:10 P.M., someone from the attorney general's office delivered papers marked "Personal and Confidential—For Eyes Only Of The Chief Justice."[15] Six of those papers added nothing to what had already been sent; in part they were a duplication. But the seventh cost Fortas his seat on the Supreme Court.

That paper was a sworn statement by Wolfson. It was in response to a grand jury subpoena *duces tecum* from the United States District Court for the District of Columbia which required him to appear at the Eglin Air Force Base in Florida on May 10, 1969, in the very midst of the hullabaloo. Wolfson had his attorneys, William O. Bittman and Austin S. Mitler, present for the interview, and he consulted with them about the statement during the interview. No one asked Fortas if he would like to have someone present, though the sole function was to inquire about the justice. There Wolfson narrated his recollection of his relationship with Fortas.

Wolfson's sworn statement continued with an account of the June meeting of the foundation in Florida. Like Fortas, Wolfson did not recall the meeting, though the minutes showed that he was present. And then, at pages six and seven of the statement, comes the blockbuster:

> Following this meeting Fortas visited me at my farm in Ocala, Florida, and, at this time, we discussed in general terms the work of the Foundation. We also discussed the Security and Exchange Commission investigation in which I was involved. Fortas again assured me that I need not worry since he still felt that these were technical violations. At this time, Fortas indicated that he had or would contact Manuel Cohen of the Security and Exchange Commission regarding this matter. Fortas indicated that he was somewhat responsible for Cohen's appointment to the Commission as Chairman.

But for this one brief passage, the statement adds nothing but a little detail or flavor to what the remaining documents already showed. However, these remarks, if Fortas made them, amounted to practicing law by expressing a legal opinion and a commitment to practice law by seeking to persuade the chairman of the Securities and Exchange Commission to follow a particular course of action. When this information came into the hands of Chief Justice Warren, coupled with the liberal payment that Fortas had received, it was open to the construction that the justice was practicing law. Warren could not have known that Rehnquist had already given the attorney general an official opinion that a justice would be subject to prosecution for practicing law unless Mitchell had hinted at something of the sort in their May 7 conversation; but Mitchell would not have needed to hint. Warren would have suspected something of the sort of the Nixon administration, for which at best he had great distrust.

Did Fortas ever say these things? On the one hand, there is no evidence that Wolfson bore Fortas any malice. Moreover, while he may not have understood the full import of his statement, he was accompanied by his two attorneys, one of them one of the best-known criminal lawyers in America, and they surely knew the import of what they were hearing and reading. As for the January 1967 meeting in Miami Beach, Wolfson expressly noted that Fortas "made no offer of assistance nor did he indicate that he would do anything one way or the other in connection with this matter."

I am confident that no deal was cut between Mitchell and Warren that if Fortas would resign, he would not be prosecuted. Mitchell would not have overtly suggested anything of the sort, and Warren, who could be vastly formidable, would not have tolerated it. But more to the point, as of the date of the Mitchell/Warren conversation, there was nothing which warranted prosecution. The air was rich with innuendo, but the conversation was on May 7, the Wolfson statement was not taken until May 10 and was not delivered until May 12, and absent the Wolfson statement there was nothing in the documentation as of May 7 which would even theoretically warrant legal proceedings.

In any case, it is clear that the chief justice thought it appropriate to report the visit and the problem to his colleagues, who met in conference with Fortas on May 13. At least some of those colleagues, quite possibly including the chief justice, thought Fortas should resign for the good of the Court. This seems at first to have been the view of Justice

Black, the senior associate. Black originally had been one of the foremost exponents and, indeed, friends of Fortas, but for whatever personal reasons, this relationship had grown strained during their years of Court service together. In private conversations from time to time, Justice Black expressed at least annoyance with Fortas, and his own extremely rigorous standards of appropriate conduct would have made him exceedingly dubious of a justice who even kept up an acquaintance with a man like Wolfson, though after private discussion with Fortas, he changed his mind. None of the justices sought to persuade Fortas not to resign. The press thundered for a Fortas resignation. On Monday, May 5, the day after Fortas issued his statement, Senator Jack Miller of Iowa called for the justice's resignation. Senator John Williams of Delaware was intensely critical. Congressman H. R. Gross of Iowa was ready with an impeachment resolution.[16] The Democrats did not support Fortas, and the *Washington Post* recommended resignation.

The next day legislative leaders met with the president. In Robert Shogan's view, the object of President Nixon and Attorney General Mitchell was to force Fortas off the Court. Nixon urged his congressional consultants to take no partisan action and to do nothing rash. He did not wish himself to be involved in an impeachment. Attorney General Mitchell was present at the meeting with the congressional leaders, and when called upon to respond as to whether the Justice Department had learned any more than the *Life* story revealed, he responded simply, "Yes."[17]

As nearly as can be discovered, Fortas discussed his decision with only two close friends, Justice William O. Douglas and Clark Clifford, a famous Washington attorney.[18] Fortas's wife (Carol Agger, still a distinguished Washington tax attorney with the onetime Fortas firm) does not recall any factors beyond the apparent ones which led to his conclusion; she has made available all private papers left by her husband that might conceivably shed any light on the matter, and none of them do. On May 14 Justice Fortas sent a letter of resignation to the chief justice.

On the basis of all evidence then known, the circumstances did not warrant a step so drastic as resignation. In 1966 Fortas accepted a lifetime subsidy for himself and for his wife after his death for serving on a Wolfson foundation, which, at the time he accepted it, had the capacity to become an immense charitable enterprise doing much good. Though no one seems to have noticed it at the time, the arrangement was not materially different from that which Andrew Carnegie made for Chief Justice

William Howard Taft forty years before. The matter is well recorded by a Taft biographer:

> William Randolph Hearst splashed across his pages the report that Taft was receiving a $10,000 annuity from the Carnegie Corporation, the interest on $200,000 in mortgage bonds of the United States Steel Corporation. Taft, as ex-President, had become involved as a result of the generosity of steelmaster Andrew Carnegie. Carnegie's will provided an income of $10,000 during Taft's life and the same amount to Mrs. Taft should she survive him. With an estate, including insurance, worth about $300,000, he did not need the money, and he hesitated to accept it. But on the urging of others, including Elihu Root, and under pressure from his wife, he had decided to take it. "Mrs. Taft wishes me to do it, and she is an interested party," Taft explained. The press rallied strongly to the Chief Justice's support. Much gratified, he observed "that no other newspapers took any part in the attack, and those which have spoken have noted its injustice." [19]

An attorney who becomes a Supreme Court justice might well find the transition from a wealthy practice to government salary awkward, though the Fortas income had been so great that perhaps supplementation was unnecessary. When it became apparent that the donor Wolfson was, in character, no Carnegie, Fortas resigned the post, canceled the arrangement, and gave the money back. He did this two years before there was any pressure of any kind to do so; his severance of the connection might well have been cause for a commendation for good conduct or, at least, thoughtful discretion.

But no exculpation would be warranted if, in fact, Fortas was in any way assisting Wolfson with his personal legal problems during 1966; such conduct would be unpardonable. Clifford, universally regarded as the soul of integrity, remembers spending the better part of a night discussing whether Fortas should resign without any hint that there was more to the story than meets the eye. Hence, the whole condemnation stems heavily from the innuendo that Attorney General Mitchell, taking the astonishingly unusual step of consulting the chief justice, must have revealed some hidden and devastating fact.

That fact must have been the information recorded in the Wolfson affidavit. Here the Department of Justice was pushing aggressively to get rid of Fortas. The *Life* story was published on May 4, and the department proceeded with all possible speed to get the subpoena from the District of Columbia grand jury and to bring Wolfson in for a statement on May 10.

That statement was back in Warren's hands by the twelfth. In 1987 I asked Justice William Brennan, the senior survivor of the Court during the resignation, whether there was some hidden something which had been suppressed then but which contributed to the resignation. He responded that he believed that there was "a letter" which had been important. No "letter" has been discovered, but the sworn statement of Wolfson amounts to the same thing and is probably what Brennan vaguely recalled.[20]

Do I believe that Fortas said what Wolfson put into his statement? No, but this is an act of faith, for who can tell what was said in a room in Ocala, Florida, between two persons on the evening of June 15, 1966? The largest reason for believing that Fortas may have been wanting in judgment but never in integrity is that Chief Justice Warren had all the facts and he never lost confidence in Fortas. Warren's file shows the care with which he etched out by hand his public statement of May 15, 1969, the day after Fortas resigned:

> Mr. Justice Fortas has announced his personal decision to resign from the Court, expressing his solicitude for the welfare of the Court as an institution.
>
> In the four years he has been here, he has been a learned and compassionate Justice. It is my sincere hope that throughout the years which lie ahead he will enjoy both success and happiness in the pursuit of his profession.

Warren was to retire himself a month later. Mrs. Warren sent Fortas a note regretting that he had not been present for the farewell ceremony. Fortas responded in a handwritten message:

> Dear Nina:
>
> How kind of you to write! I thought it would be best to be absent— but our hearts joined in the tributes that were paid to both of you!
>
> God bless both of you. I hope we shall soon see you.
>
> Abe

Only a week later, it was Fortas's birthday, and Mrs. Warren sent him a birthday cake. Once again he wrote:

> Dear Nina, Dear Friend—
>
> How very kind of you to send me a Justice's Birthday Cake! It makes the day much brighter. My very, very best to you and your family.
>
> Abe

A few months later, the Warrens came to the Fortas home for dinner, and Warren wrote to "Dear Carol and Abe" of the "great pleasure" of seeing "both of you again." A few months later in connection with some other matter he wrote Fortas again asking Fortas to join him for lunch and giving him free rein to pick a time.[21] Earl Warren would not have maintained that kind of a relationship with someone he thought lacking in integrity.

Granted that Justice Fortas helped feed the furnace in which he was consumed. It was bad judgment to get into the Wolfson situation in the first place; it led to grave loss of public confidence, and while the particular form that loss took could not be anticipated, some trouble might have been expected. Fortas did not have to respond to the *Life* request for a statement. He did not have to issue a statement after the *Life* article appeared. But in both instances, he chose to make a statement but only a partial one, and his incomplete disclosures were disastrous. He more than made up for this elision in his resignation statement of May 14, a four-page letter to the chief justice. Here he narrated his association with Wolfson as a client, the purposes of the foundation, the financial arrangement for himself and Mrs. Fortas, the payment, the Ocala meeting, his termination of the association, and his return of the 1966 fee. He expressly declared that he had had no part "in any legal, administrative or judicial matter affecting Mr. Wolfson or anyone associated with him." Yet, he went on:

> It is my opinion, however, that the public controversy relating to my association with the Foundation is likely to continue and adversely affect the work and position of the Court, absent my resignation. In these circumstances, it seems clear to me that it is not my duty to remain on the Court, but rather to resign in the hope that this will enable the Court to proceed with its vital work free from extraneous stress.[22]

It was a sad moment for Fortas admirers. Fortas found himself in this situation because a felt need for income ran ahead of judgment. If the Wolfson statement was a misunderstanding, Fortas nevertheless had exposed himself to that kind of misunderstanding. Arthur Freund, a St. Louis lawyer of the time, a gentleman par excellence, and a deep admirer of Fortas, said, "I didn't know that Abe was a Geldfresser," a Yiddish word for one who eats money, an avaricious person.[23] James Wechsler, in the *New York Post*, also an admirer, wrote:

Abe Fortas has been a distinguished member of the high court. When he was named to the Court, he was presumably accepting a large financial sacrifice. But the going rate of $60,000 is hardly a sweatshop wage and, for men who care about the traditions of the law, elevation to this tribunal is the ultimate triumph in life. The heartbreaking enigma is why anyone who has achieved this eminence would risk everything by the tawdry Wolfson involvement. His defenders will say that Fortas must have been convinced that there was no impropriety in the association; his critics must retort that this judgment reveals a moral astigmatism.[24]

The *New York Times* welcomed the resignation with traditional sanctimony, stating that "a judge not only has to be innocent of any wrongdoing but he also has to be above reproach."[25] The *Washington Post* more directly said that the public explanation "is not good enough."[26] In an interview with the executive editor of the *Post*, Fortas said that he saw no sinister plot in the events leading to his resignation:

> It's just as if an automobile hit me as I stepped off the curb. I wouldn't think the driver is a fiend or an evil man. I'm not the kind of man who looks for that kind of thing.
> There was something . . . a quick, simple series of events that occurred at a moment in time, June, 1966. The return of the check—I really delayed there just as an act of humanity. I had closed my mind to it all. No hits, no runs, no errors. And here it comes back to haunt me.

Fortas explained that he decided to resign as soon as he perceived that the controversy would "go on and on." "We've got the Vietnam War and all the disorder. You can't expect to have all that going on, plus the confrontation over this and expect the Supreme Court to go on."[27]

The choice of a successor for Justice Fortas occupies the remainder of these pages.

II

Haynsworth and the Circuit Judgeship

Clement Haynsworth of Greenville, South Carolina, was old-line America and old-line law. His mother's ancestors came to this continent in the seventeenth century, and on his father's side, Haynsworth, born in 1912, was descended from Revolutionary patriots.[1] He was the fifth generation in direct succession of Haynsworth lawyers in South Carolina. His great-great-grandfather, William Haynsworth, was admitted to practice in the courts of South Carolina in 1813. His great-grandfather was killed at Second Manassas. His grandfather, Harry J. Haynsworth, married the daughter of Dr. James Clement Furman, a Baptist minister and the president of Furman University at Greenville.[2] His great-great-grandfather originated and his great-grandfather was the first president of that university, a school which continued to be a lifetime object of his bounty. In short, there can't be an older "Old South" than Judge Haynsworth.

Haynsworth had a little preparatory school training at the Darlington School in Rome, Georgia, before graduating there on June 1, 1929; he was an above-average student with a good reputation at the school. He then attended Furman, graduating with an A.B. degree summa cum laude in 1933. From there he went to the Harvard Law School, the third-generation Haynsworth to do so, and graduated in 1936 fifty-first in a class of 399 students.

Upon leaving Harvard, Haynsworth returned to Greenville where he joined the firm whose senior partners were his grandfather and his father. The firm's work grew into a major corporate practice for this upper part of South Carolina, with Haynsworth regarded both a thoroughgoing professional and a great business getter. He was engaged in intelligence work for the navy during World War II and in the course of those years became acquainted with Dorothy Merry Barkley. Mrs. Barkley for some years had experienced an unhappy marriage; in 1946 she was divorced and soon after married Haynsworth. Theirs was an extraordinarily happy marriage for forty years; in elegant southern style, Mrs. Haynsworth was generally referred to, both by her husband and others, as "Miss Dorothy."

During the Korean War, Haynsworth also served part-time for two years with the Wage Stabilization Board for the Atlanta region. Politically, he was a registered Democrat, not very active; but he had been a "Democrat for Eisenhower." After going to the bench, he limited his political activity to voting.[3]

Correspondence of 1956 shows a warm relationship between President Eisenhower and Haynsworth's cousins Mr. and Mrs. Alestair G. Furman, Jr., who were invited to participate in the inaugural functions "as the personal guests of Mamie and myself." In 1957 Haynsworth was nominated by President Eisenhower for the United States Court of Appeals for the Fourth Circuit.

When Clement Haynsworth went to the fourth circuit court of appeals in 1957, there were three judges on the court. These three were the fastest appeals team in the country; in their court it took about four months from the filing of the typical case to a decision.[4] Haynsworth learned under a master, Chief Judge John J. Parker of North Carolina, who became his intimate friend.

Between 1957 and 1969, when Haynsworth was nominated to the Supreme Court, the number of cases in the fourth circuit quintupled, and the number of judges had doubled. Haynsworth had become chief judge and had been a good administrator of a hardworking court; despite the disproportionately increased workload, the fourth circuit was still one of the most efficient courts in the country.[5]

The most visible measure of a judge's work is in his opinions. By 1987 Haynsworth had written about 640 opinions for his court, including a spattering of dissents and concurrences; he did not dissent or concur very often, sharing a deeply held view of most lawyers that this side talk does not help anyone very much. In 1969 his total number of opinions was, of course, much smaller, but it is still too voluminous to do more than sample. Mention of a few cases will show what he had been doing in his first twelve years.[6]

Haynsworth's first opinion, in May 1957, was a patent case on a tobacco harvester, memorable only because it was his first case.[7] An early more important matter held that suits against counties, cities, or other lesser governmental units could be brought in federal courts and should not be limited to state courts.[8] This was a technical but significant decision which was broadly praised in legal publications around the country. In yet another early case, he held that federal courts could not, under the civil rights statutes, enjoin state criminal proceedings, but he reserved the possibility of such injunctions in extraordinary instances to avoid grave and irreparable injury to citizens.[9] The line he took is similar to that later adopted by the Supreme Court.

We shall never know how Haynsworth would have dealt with certain important problems if he had had final authority. As a lower court judge, he felt himself bound by the Supreme Court's higher authority even when he found it distasteful. For example, he was not very sympathetic to the practice of a government agency, when charged with wrongdoing, hiding behind rules that the government could not be sued. He reluctantly decided a case in favor of the Park Service and against a citizen who appeared to have been wronged, even though he would have liked to give "a more restrictive role" to the government position; he had concluded that the Supreme Court seemed to be "leading us in the other direction."[10] What he would have done as a Supreme Court justice when he was in a position to change the rule, we will never know.

On the other hand, when he felt that the Supreme Court itself would no longer follow a particular rule, he felt free to depart from it. He thus gave an opinion extending the right of habeas corpus in a bold fashion which Chief Justice Warren later expressly praised, noting that the Supreme Court was "in complete agreement" with Judge Haynsworth's position.[11] In two other exceptionally fine opinions just before his nomination to the Supreme Court, he took an advanced position on the proper test for insanity in criminal cases, and he set forth the rules to determine when there is sufficient evidence to go to a jury.[12] The latter case has come to be standard instruction for students in law schools.

In the great conflagration in the Senate in 1969, none of this good judicial work was of any consequence at all. The brickbats and the kudos were for his labor and civil rights opinions. The AFL-CIO's appraisal of Judge Haynsworth's labor cases includes a list of seven that were regarded by the AFL-CIO as antilabor, in which the Supreme Court's reversals were unanimous in six cases and almost so in the seventh.[13] Some of his labor opinions were not criticized by the AFL-CIO, one was described as a close question, and in another the labor statement reports that his decision "is plainly correct." However, the prime focus was on the reversals. The hyperbole of the time was excessive if meant to suggest that Judge Haynsworth was systematically deciding all cases against unions.[14] However, it is certainly true that the Nixon administration in choosing Judge Haynsworth was not appointing a prolabor judge.

A labor case in which Judge Haynsworth wrote the opinion presented the question of when authorization cards signed by union members could be used to give a union collective bargaining rights where, due to unfair labor practices, it was impractical to hold an election. Judge Haynsworth held that the cards could not, at least in an ordinary case, be used for this purpose. Most of the other federal courts took the opposite point of view, and the Supreme Court reversed the fourth circuit position.[15]

Two civil rights cases were severely criticized by the Haynsworth opponents. One was *Simkins v. Moses H. Cone Memorial Hospital,* in which the issue was whether a hospital which received large amounts of federal funds could refuse to serve black patients.[16] The majority of the fourth circuit said no; Judge Haynsworth dissented because the hospital had been privately established. The second major attack was on *Griffin v. Board of Supervisors.*[17] Joseph Rauh, speaking for the civil rights opponents of Haynsworth, said at the hearings, "I guess if there's one thing that Judge Haynsworth did that more than anything else infuriates the civil rights movement, I would say it is *Griffin.*"[18] The *Griffin* case arose from Prince Edward County, Virginia, party to one of the original cases in which segregation was declared unconstitutional by the Supreme Court in 1954. Prince Edward County responded by closing its public schools and subsidizing private all-white schools. Judge Haynsworth's opinion held that the legality of this system should first be decided by the Virginia Supreme Court. The United States Supreme Court, in substance, removed the case from the court of appeals, held that there was no need to wait any longer, and ordered the reopening of the public schools.

There was also a great tide of Haynsworth decisions that were favorable to civil rights.[19] Haynsworth had voted to speed integration of a golf course, voided the discriminatory discharge of a black teacher, eliminated district boundaries intended to perpetuate segregation, and held that both teacher and student assignments could not be made on the basis of race. Nonetheless, what the Senate saw was *Cone* and *Griffin.* If the Nixon administration had wanted to choose a judge zealous for civil rights, it certainly would not have chosen Haynsworth. If it wished to choose a judge temperate on civil rights, it might well have chosen him.

There was one extremely unpleasant episode during the Haynsworth judgeship which was to cast a long shadow. It involved a vending business named Carolina Vend-a-Matic, a corporation organized in 1950 by six partners of the Haynsworth firm, including Haynsworth, plus a local Greenville businessman. The business operated food vending machines in numerous business places and factories, including textile plants. As of January 1, 1957, each shareholder had twenty-four shares for which each had paid about $3,000. Bank loans were financed by the shareholders, and the business grew. With slight changes of personnel in the group, the company was reorganized in January 1960, when Wade Dennis became its president. Sales rose between 1961 and 1963 from $1.6 million to $3.1 million. Bank loans climbed to a half-million dollars by 1961.

As of 1963, the company had equipment in three Deering-Milliken textile plants, though none with the Darlington plant of that company. In 1963 Deering-Milliken constructed a new plant and took bids for vending machines from eight companies. Vend-a-Matic's was thought to be best, and it got the contract. In June 1963 bids were sought by another and larger Deering-Milliken plant. On this one, Vend-a-Matic lost. In November 1963 it lost another one. The three Deering-Milliken plants in operation in 1963 furnished about $100,000, or 3 percent of the gross Vend-a-Matic sales for the year. Some nine separate vending companies had machines in one or more of the Deering-Milliken plants.

In 1957 Haynsworth resigned from the office of company vice president, but he remained as a director until in 1963 the Federal Judicial Conference asked that no judge should serve as officer or director of any corporation, at which time he resigned. The company sold out to ARA, a national vending company, in 1963. Haynsworth liquidated his interest for approximately $450,000.[20]

In 1963 a labor case involving the Darlington plant of Deering-Milliken came before Haynsworth. Deering-Milliken and Company was a determinedly antilabor employer. The court of appeals, three to two with Judge Haynsworth joining the majority opinion, held that the employer had an absolute right to close an individual mill for antiunion purposes, a decision which the Supreme Court limitedly reversed; the Supreme Court held that a multiunit employer could, if it wished, close its entire operation for any purpose but that it could not select out an individual unit for closure for antiunion purposes.[21]

On December 17, 1963, a Textile Workers Union (TWUA) attorney wrote the presiding judge of the fourth circuit, Simon E. Sobeloff, concerning an anonymous telephone call the union had received about an alleged bribe of Judge Haynsworth; the fact that the call was limited to an alleged bribe and nothing else later become of critical importance. What the bribe was supposed to be was never identified; supposedly it had something to do with Vend-a-Matic and the Deering-Milliken plants.

Judge Sobeloff immediately undertook an investigation. On February 6, 1964, the union attorney, in a letter to Sobeloff, withdrew the charge, saying, "Since we now know that the allegation made to our union was inaccurate, we know that the trouble was unnecessary." Haynsworth asked that the file be transmitted to Attorney General Robert F. Kennedy for review, and on February 28, 1964, Kennedy wrote Sobeloff: "Your thorough and complete investigation reflects that the charges were without foundation. I share your expression of complete confidence in Judge Haynsworth."[22]

III

The Supreme Court Appointment

Senator Ernest Hollings, Democrat of South Carolina, whom Attorney General Mitchell regarded as a "great guy," was for Haynsworth for the Fortas vacancy.[1] Hollings had become acquainted with Mitchell through Nelson Rockefeller, and when Hollings finished his term as governor of South Carolina, Mitchell had hoped to have Hollings join his New York law firm. However, upon the death of Senator Olin Johnson of South Carolina, Hollings scratched the return to private practice in favor of going to the Senate. Thus, Haynsworth was on the list that Mitchell assembled in 1969 when he was considering the chief justiceship nomination for a successor to Earl Warren. Warren Burger was selected for that nomination, and the rest of the names on the list were sent to him and, in addition, to Hollings for consideration as a replacement for Fortas.

On May 28, 1969, Senator Hollings met at the White House with President Nixon and recommended Judge Haynsworth for the Supreme Court vacancy. The president asked that Hollings detail Haynsworth's qualifications. Hollings reminded the president that Nixon had met Haynsworth "several years ago with our late friend, Charlie Daniel of Greenville, when Charlie was sworn into the Senate." Haynsworth had been a great jurist, Hollings said, and "he has brought the Fourth Circuit to the highest degree of administrative efficiency that the Court has ever enjoyed."[2]

On the same day, Haynsworth wrote Senator Strom Thurmond of South Carolina forwarding a biographical sketch. Haynsworth said, "I am giving some thought to your suggestion that letters from judges and resolutions of bar associations might be of assistance." He added that he had some reluctance for fear of appearing to use his office to campaign.

Two days later he wrote Hollings in response to a copy of the Hollings-Nixon letter, saying, "If the President is looking for experienced judges, however, I am in the rather enviable position of having as much as twelve years experience as an appellate judge, while so far avoiding attaining a state of very advanced years." Haynsworth's attitude hardened into resolve, and on June 9 he wrote Senator Thurmond again saying that he was "consistently rejecting, though with as much graciousness as I can, all the proffers of assistance in the form of letters or resolutions." [3]

On July 1, 1969, Attorney General Mitchell called J. Edgar Hoover, director of the Federal Bureau of Investigation (FBI). He told Hoover that the president was considering the appointment of Haynsworth to the Supreme Court, and he asked for a preliminary check so that something would be in the record if and when needed. He wanted this extremely confidential. Hoover directed the agent in charge in the fourth circuit to give him a rundown on Haynsworth's ability and standing without making any outside inquiries, and this plan satisfied the attorney general. A response from Roland Trent, the agent in charge at Columbia, South Carolina, described Haynsworth as the "foremost jurist in the area, very conservative and definitely in favor of law and order." The report noted that Haynsworth had a slight lisp but was considered to have a brilliant mind and that there was no derogatory information. Hoover reported to the attorney general at once. An FBI file report of the same date noted that Haynsworth was regarded as "an ardent supporter of the FBI." [4]

At that time, there had been no Haynsworth conversations with either Senator Hollings or Senator Thurmond. However, Hollings had made some announcement in Washington earlier that Haynsworth was under consideration and that Hollings was recommending him.

After the dust had settled almost a year later, the best comprehensive review of the Haynsworth appointment came in the March 1970 *Fortune* magazine. There were 150 names on the list prepared by Attorney General Mitchell and his deputy, Richard Kleindienst, of those who "merited consideration" for the chief justice nomination. The list was pared to ten before the administration chose Burger; Haynsworth and two other later appointees, Harry Blackmun and Lewis Powell, were among them. To fill the Fortas vacancy, Mitchell and the president went over the same list with very few additions. [5]

Mitchell met Haynsworth for the first time in March 1969, and the attorney general told Haynsworth that he knew a great deal about him. In late June the two conferred at the Homestead resort in Virginia where the attorney general was delivering an address to the fourth circuit conference. At this meeting, Mitchell said that he had read Haynsworth's opinions, and Haynsworth then realized that this had been in connection with a survey for the Supreme Court appointment. The attorney general asked about financial investments. Haynsworth did not have the details with him but told Mitchell in general what they were. Mitchell asked about the availability of income tax returns, and Haynsworth said he would be glad to supply them. The whole conversation took about an hour. There was no commitment on the part of President Nixon by Mitchell, but obviously the appointment was what Mitchell had in mind.[6]

Before the conversations with Mitchell there had been some rumor about an appointment; retired justice Tom Clark had been at the same conference and had said in one executive session that he thought Haynsworth was going to be appointed to the Supreme Court. "Tom was very pleased about the prospect," Haynsworth reported. This was the first time that Haynsworth learned that the consideration was truly serious.[7]

Haynsworth did not know whether Senator Thurmond had anything to do with pushing the appointment. Senator Joseph Tydings of Maryland was present at the fourth circuit conference. He came up to Mitchell and Haynsworth and said to Mitchell in Haynsworth's presence, "I am so glad I'm here because we've got to do something about getting the judge on the Supreme Court."[8] Tydings was to have a 180-degree change of position.

Johnnie Mac Walters, assistant attorney general for the Tax Division, was an old friend whom Haynsworth had known since Walters was a young man in college. On June 30 Haynsworth sent his 1957–68 tax returns to Walters, and on July 2 he sent Walters a number of his opinions. On that same day, Walters sent to Mitchell a memorandum concerning Haynsworth's tax returns, which he found all in good order. Walters also reported in regard to Haynsworth's income from earlier days that he had received substantial dividends and a good sum from his law practice. The returns of the past five years showed that Haynsworth had received no income other than his salary as a judge, dividends and interests on investments, and rentals on some small parcels of leased real estate.[9]

On August 1, 1969, Haynsworth wrote his cousin Elizabeth Hirsh in Portland, Oregon. He said he did not believe that he was firmly settled on as the appointee but he was aware that he was in the news, "and I don't get in the least upset when *Newsweek* showers me with compliments such as gray, bland, hardworking professional but no intellect" or "when charged by Roy Wilkins as being a segregationist." He continued, "Still, the press reports are not too far from the mark and I am highly flattered that the matter has gone as far as it has." He added that he was happy at what he was doing and would not be a bit disappointed if someone else was chosen; he "certainly would not welcome the personal disruption such an appointment would make." [10]

Haynsworth was aware that the Justice Department had begun with a long list, cut it down to two or three, and that he was the one chosen, but he never knew who the others were. Between the time of the June conversation with Mitchell and the appointment, there was at least a fifty-day span. During that period, Haynsworth heard nothing from either Mitchell or Nixon, but he did hear from time to time from Walters. Walters reported a request by Mitchell to convey the message that everything was fine but that the administration was waiting for the right moment. [11]

On August 13 the Senate Republican leader, Senator Everett Dirksen, leaked the upcoming nomination to the press, and five days later the president made it. Quick confirmation was expected. Two of the eventual foes lined up immediately in support, Senator Robert Griffin of Michigan, the assistant Republican leader, and Senator Tydings of Maryland, a close family friend. Dirksen's death in early September was a great loss—in retrospect, probably fatal—to Haynsworth's confirmation. The new Senate Republican leader, Hugh Scott of Pennsylvania, ended up as a Haynsworth opponent; and the new assistant Republican leader, Senator Griffin, became vociferously hostile.

Two days before the appointment, President Nixon called; this was the only occasion of any direct contact between the two men before the appointment was made. The call came at the dinner hour, when the judge would ordinarily not have been disturbed. The interruption, "Will the judge take a call from the president?" proved to be an exception. While the name of Haynsworth was being spoken of, there had been some talk in the press of the Darlington Mills matter, and Haynsworth had reported on that topic to the Justice Department through Walters. Nixon referred to the Darlington inquiry when he spoke to Haynsworth on the phone. He said that he had reviewed that file and was going to mention it in his announcement because he thought he would kill that bird at the time. [12]

On August 18, 1969, the president did nominate Haynsworth. The president's press secretary announced that Attorney General Mitchell had told Haynsworth several weeks earlier that he was under consideration. The president's statement applauded Haynsworth's "demonstrated judicial temperament, balance, impartiality and fairness" and noted that at the age of fifty-six he was eminently qualified as a lawyer, a scholar, and an intellectual.[13] It was President Nixon's policy not to clear Supreme Court appointments with the Republican National Committee, the American Bar Association (ABA), or (allegedly) with senators, although Senator Hollings had been a strong Haynsworth backer. According to press accounts, Senator Thurmond, also of South Carolina, had recommended the state's former senator and governor Donald S. Russell, but Thurmond was said to be content with the appointment.[14] Senator James O. Eastland of Mississippi, chairman of the Senate Judiciary Committee, set the hearing on the nomination for September 9.

The president did take the unusual step of releasing a statement concerning the *Darlington* problem. When the appointment was made, there began an accumulation of memoranda in the files of the Justice Department supporting Haynsworth's conduct in *Vend-a-Matic*. One of these of August 28 was by then Assistant Attorney General Rehnquist.[15]

On August 18 Haynsworth wrote President Nixon accepting the nomination and forwarding to him a brief formal press release he had issued: "The President has highly honored me in his announcement of my appointment to the Supreme Court. For his trust in me, I am deeply grateful. I will strive earnestly to justify his confidence by a rededication of myself to service in the administration of justice."[16]

On that day, Professor Charles Alan Wright of the University of Texas Law School wrote an exultant letter to Haynsworth. In it he quoted Judge Charles Wyzanski of Boston: "Being asked to serve on the Supreme Court would be like being invited to spend the night with Cleopatra. First, of course, you would accept. Second, you would have doubts about your ability to perform. And third, after you had done it you would find that it wasn't nearly as much fun as you thought it would be."[17] Professor Bernard Ward, also of the University of Texas, on August 19 sent a handwritten note to the judge: "Now thank we all our God!"[18]

Letters of congratulations from fellow judges flooded in: Judge Robert Ainsworth of the fifth circuit, Judge Sterry Waterman of the second circuit, Judge Alfred Murrah of the tenth circuit, Judge Carl McGowan of the District of Columbia circuit. Another letter was from Jerome ("Buddy") Cooper, a leading union lawyer of Birmingham, Alabama, who had been the first clerk of Justice Hugo Black: "There are issues and points of politics and a philosophy on which you and I might find some disagreement but deep in my being I know with certainty that you will bring to the Supreme Court capacity, a degree of integrity and a devotion to our country." [19]

The first public response to the nomination was largely favorable. The *U.S. News and World Report* assessed Haynsworth's judicial record as establishing him to be "a moderate in judicial philosophy." It anticipated a conservative tilt to the new Court, though on racial matters "no major shift is foreseen." It reported that Haynsworth had ruled that freedom-of-choice desegregation plans would be "acceptable only if the choice is free in the practical context of its exercise." He had said, "If there are extraneous pressures which deprive the choice of its freedom, the school board may be required to adopt affirmative measures to counter them." He also had directed a school board to come up with "some minimal, objective timetable for a faculty desegregation." In the criminal field, he had dissented from a ruling invalidating the North Carolina death penalty and had favored giving the police more power in search and seizure cases, but at the same time had enlarged the right to use habeas corpus. In regard to the standard of insanity in criminal cases, he had endorsed the modern criteria and rejected the older and more conservative tests still prevalent in the country. [20]

In a handwritten note of August 24, retired justice Tom Clark said, "We read of your appointment and were elated." Clark offered to lend him a law clerk to get through the first matters, and Haynsworth in quick response accepted. A warm handwritten note was sent by Justice Byron White on September 10, 1969. [21]

Time magazine anticipated that Haynsworth would be a good choice to carry out Nixon's wish to steer the Supreme Court away from the Warren Court "activism." It noted also the political advantages of the appointment. *Time* assessed the opposition as "not as outraged as might have been expected." [22]

On August 21 Haynsworth wrote a three-page letter to Attorney General Mitchell reporting "a few things that have been done which bear upon problems being encountered." Three law clerks from the fourth circuit had discussed matters of his civil rights positions with friends at the NAACP. "Clarence Mitchell asked to see them and Dan Grove has reported to me that Mitchell left the meeting with an acknowledgment of the fact that he was shaken in his earlier position. He requested that a letter analyzing the cases be written to him." The same friends were participants in a CBS broadcast to the same effect. He reported that Professor G. W. Foster, Jr., of the University of Wisconsin Law School, a strong civil rights figure, was ready to help. "Joe Tydings called me to tell me that he would do all that he could to support the nomination, as I knew he would. We have known Joe's mother for many years and have had very frequent contact with him." Tydings undertook to speak to senators Philip A. Hart of Michigan and Birch Bayh of Indiana when they returned. In an undated note in response to a note from Haynsworth on August 22, Chief Justice Burger said, "As I suggested yesterday, let your friends carry the ball and try to ignore the nonsense, for that is what it is."[23]

Before the September hearing, the country had begun to be heard from. The American Bar Association found Haynsworth "highly qualified." In an illustration of the clouded crystal ball, University of Chicago law professor Philip Kurland told the world that "he's not going to be unacceptable to anybody."[24] The appointment was regarded by some as a political coup for President Nixon and his "Southern strategy" to increase Republican support in the South in the 1970 and 1972 elections.[25]

Savage criticism quickly began. The *Vend-a-Matic* matter led to hard talk. Perhaps the most vicious of the newspaper columns was that by Frank Mankiewicz and Tom Braden, published on September 3. "He decided an important case in favor of a company doing $100,000 worth of business a year with his company, an act in which he says—incredibly—that he saw no impropriety and sees none now." Also, he "participated along with Attorney General John Mitchell and the White House in a shabby attempt to make it seem that Attorney General Robert Kennedy approved of his behavior, a claim they knew to be false when they made it."[26]

George Meany, president of the AFL-CIO, writing Senator Eastland, said that Haynsworth was "not fit to be an Associate Justice of the Supreme Court."[27] The unfitness charge by Meany and other unions centered on that same 1963 case, in which, at the time, the union had withdrawn the charge and Haynsworth, Braden and Markiewicz to the contrary notwithstanding, had been expressly cleared and applauded by then Attorney General Kennedy. William Pollock, head of the Textile Workers Union which had made and withdrawn the charges six years earlier, now reversed the union's stance again, concluding that there has been a conflict of interest.

In reviewing the matter, *Time* reported that the civil rights groups had been opposed to Haynsworth's appointment from the first and that Meany at the AFL-CIO had concluded to "put everything into blocking the nomination" after receiving a report on labor decisions from the organization's associate general counsel Thomas E. Harris. The report continued that the AFL-CIO, at the peak of its anti-Haynsworth drive, had forty full-time lobbyists deployed on the case.[28] Between the date of the Dirksen "leak" and the actual nomination, Meany sent a private wire to the president urging that the nomination not be made.[29] Just after Labor Day, Meany met with Andrew J. Biemiller, the AFL-CIO's legislative director, and a few others and asked how many votes they could get in opposition. Biemiller replied that there were eight. Meany asked whether this number could be tripled, and Biemiller replied, "We can double it certainly, triple it maybe." Meany then made "the key decision." "All right," he said, "we're in it all the way."[30] The three who were actually to lead the opposition were Senator Bayh, Biemiller, and Joseph L. Rauh, Jr., counsel to the Leadership Conference on Civil Rights.

Those groups needed a leader and allegedly went first to Senator Hart of Michigan who begged off because he had championed Fortas. There was some thought of Senator Kennedy, but according to *Newsweek* a labor aide said, "We couldn't use Teddy to wage a fight on an ethical issue."[31] The final choice was Bayh. Civil rights groups joined the unions in opposition, complaining that Haynsworth had joined in several freedom-of-choice desegregation plans. The NAACP's president, Roy Wilkins, aligned with George Meany in committing to oppose Haynsworth's confirmation.

At an early stage, I was asked by Senator Eastland to testify at the first hearing on the matter of the law of disqualification, and other persons similarly were invited to appear on civil rights and other matters. A question later put to Judge Haynsworth was, "Who was making the decision that there ought to be some good solid affirmative testimony at that hearing and that it was necessary that the matter would not be perfunctory? Was that a decision by you, was it a decision by Senator Eastland or his staff, was it the Department of Justice?"[32]

Haynsworth did not know who made the decision to put on a positive hearing. Shortly before the proceedings were scheduled to start, he was invited to Washington at the request of Senator Hollings to meet members of the Senate, and he did make the rounds and shake a number of hands. He saw senators Jacob Javits, Margaret Chase Smith, Daniel

Inouye, Mike Mansfield, Kennedy, and others. All were extremely pleasant. At the time Haynsworth had doubts about Javits. "His welcome to me could not have been more gracious or warmer, and, indeed, he said that he was much inclined to vote for me." Javits told Haynsworth that if after he had reviewed his opinions he had no doubts on the race question, he would be all for him. He also met Senator Scott who said that he would be all for him.

At the same time, he became aware that some labor representatives were seeking someone to head up the fight against him. They could find no one; Senator Hart had refused. Haynsworth felt that the talk that he was a "strict constructionist" and might not have an open mind on racial issues led to some concern. Professor William Van Alstyne of the Duke University School of Law, thought of by Haynsworth as a "very liberal-minded, able professor," wrote the *New York Times* that Haynsworth was not "the kind of moss-back strict constructionist to which they should object." Haynsworth believed that it was the labor flare-up that caused the decision "by someone" that the committee should have some affirmative witnesses.

The practical result of Dirksen's death was to delay the hearings a week. The judge's cousin Harry Haynsworth had come up simply for the ride and an interesting experience; he was to see it through as the judge's hardest-working aide, taking a three-month leave without compensation from his law office. During that week Haynsworth went home and waited. During this period he thought there might be a few questions since he had been asked to supply much material, but he had no anticipation of the rising storm. The day before the hearings were supposed to open, Harry had been at the Justice Department in Walters's office when he was handed a copy of the hearings on Chief Justice Burger, which Walters had been studying, and was told that was what to expect. This was to prepare the judge on the way to avoid answering questions as to how he would rule on particular matters without antagonizing the senator who asked the question.

The *AFL-CIO News* on August 30 amplified the labor opposition, and the AFL-CIO began to put up what it described itself as "one of our biggest fights on the Hill this year." In this organization newspaper Meany reported that the *Darlington* decision cost the jobs of 500 workers; its later reversal by the Supreme Court assertedly gave them the chance to receive either compensation or jobs. The account reviewed the *Vend-a-*

Matic case and TWUA president Pollock's reversal of his position. AFL-CIO counsel Harris said of Haynsworth: "He sat on five labor cases that went to the Supreme Court. In all five, he voted against the union. All five cases were reversed by the Supreme Court and only one Supreme Court judge in one case voted the way that Judge Haynsworth did in these cases."[33]

On the same day as the *AFL-CIO News* story, the *Washington Post* editorially called for close examination of the *Vend-a-Matic* matter by the Senate committee. The editorial proclaimed the line which was to be the focus of the hearings. The 1963 clearance of the charge against Haynsworth was minimized because it had been asserted that Deering-Milliken had given a contract to Vend-a-Matic while the case was pending as a bribe to a federal judge; this charge was generally acknowledged to be a worthless one; the only contract the company had obtained had been by competitive bidding.

But, said the *Post*, there was an independent question as to whether a judge could properly sit at all in a case involving a party where he owns stock in a supplier. This, said the *Post*, was a matter of "propriety," not of law, and the *Post* urged the committee to consider whether Judge Haynsworth had proceeded "with discretion and propriety." A complete review of the entire file of the Sobeloff investigation in 1964 makes it apparent that there was no serious attention given to the question of ownership of stock in a supplier, the so-called conflict of interest. Until 1969 when someone dug the question up and attempted to use it as a distinction, no one had ever supposed that there was anything to investigate on this score.

On Sunday, August 31, George Meany was interviewed on the ABC television program "Issues and Answers." A portion of the program was on Haynsworth's appointment, and Meany was explicit that the AFL-CIO intended to try to induce members of the Senate to vote against confirmation. He declared that his objections were based on the labor decisions and also on a question of ethics. In *Vend-a-Matic*, Meany charged, Haynsworth lacked "the legal ethics of straight-forward honesty." Meany stressed his view that the attorney general's letter and the previous investigation absolved the judge of any claim of bribery but not of conflict of interest.

In response, Assistant Attorney General Walters began actively assisting in the campaign to get Haynsworth affirmed. He got the letters from Sobeloff and Attorney General Kennedy to Senator Hollings in connection with *Vend-a-Matic*. Walters wanted Attorney General Mitchell to call on Senator Tydings to ask him to introduce Haynsworth to Senator Hart and other liberal senators. He also assigned himself the duty of reviewing other hearings to see what could be expected. The most pointed note in this list was one to "induce Senator Thurmond to remain as silent as possible"; Senator Thurmond was then regarded as the leading racist in the Senate, and his support could not improve the Haynsworth image.

Walters wanted the judge to be prepared to answer extremely specific questions on *Vend-a-Matic* and to be able to lay out all the facts. He should also have specific answers to all possible questions on his investment and financial interests and a list of any memberships that the judge might have in any organizations. Walters wanted to think about whether any questions might arise in connection with Miss Dorothy's divorce and subsequent marriage to Haynsworth, and he noted that the judge must ask himself, "Are there any skeletons?" He made a note to check with former justice Tom Clark to see whether he could be helpful on any matters. Walters was also making notes on who the witnesses should be. It was Walters who planned which senators Haynsworth should meet before the hearing started, even to the details of the times and the places. On September 3 Walters noted that the Tydings office was looking for an analysis of Haynsworth's labor decisions and that Senator John McClellan's office wanted a report on his criminal cases.[34]

A year after his defeat, Haynsworth did not know the relative roles of the Justice Department and Senator Eastland in the planning of the hearing. Eastland had forwarded a request for financial information from senators Bayh and Hart and later from senators Hart and Tydings. It was not until Haynsworth got to Washington on the day after the death of Senator Dirksen that he first met Assistant Attorney General William H. Rehnquist or anyone else in the Justice Department other than Walters. It was thereafter Rehnquist who headed up the department program at the Senate. Haynsworth also met Richard Kleindienst who, playing the role of devil's advocate, gave him an hour-and-a-half grilling with adverse questions. This was a kind of a moot court, and both Haynsworth and Kleindienst were pleased with it.[35]

IV

The Judiciary Committee

Darlington *and Disqualification*

With the hearing date set for September 9, Haynsworth came to Washington, only to discover that Senator Dirksen's death had delayed the proceedings a week. Two of the witnesses coming to the originally scheduled hearing were Charles Alan Wright and I. The judge reached me by phone just before I was to board the plane. But he could not stop Wright, who said that it was "the longest trip he ever had made for a hamburger" after he turned around and flew back to Austin, Texas.[1]

During the delay, two top officers of the Department of Justice who were to be the principal figures from the department supporting Haynsworth's appointment went into action. Assistant Attorney General Walters took his fellow South Carolinian in to visit with Attorney General Mitchell.[2] Assistant Attorney General Rehnquist issued an opinion to the Senate Judiciary Committee declaring that far from being disqualified, Haynsworth had a "duty to sit" in the *Darlington* case and that far from being legally barred from participating, he was legally bound to participate. This opinion was jointly announced by Senate Judiciary Committee chairman Eastland and the ranking Republican member of the committee, Senator Roman L. Hruska of Nebraska. The two senators described the criticism of Haynsworth as "utterly baseless" and declared that the clearance by Attorney General Kennedy had covered not merely the charge of bribery but also any questions of "propriety and ethical conduct" as well.[3]

During August labor made vigorous attacks on the Vend-a-Matic matter, and on September 3 when Congress returned after a recess, labor and civil rights groups began to buttonhole senators.[4] The hearings were prefaced with thirty-five pages of documents. These included the Justice

Department records on the Deering-Milliken investigation of 1963 and a letter from senators Hart and Tydings, both members of the committee, with detailed questions as to the Haynsworth interest in Vend-a-Matic and that company's business relations with Deering-Milliken.[5] As Biemiller put it, "Abe Fortas was there all the time. We just repeated what people had said about him."[6] Bayh personally, upon his return from Europe, spent hours going over tax returns and brokerage accounts that Haynsworth supplied.

By September 16 the initiative had passed to the opposition and was never recovered; but on Monday, September 15, the judge still looked strong. Senator Javits, Republican of New York, said that while he probably would vote against the nomination, he believed that Haynsworth would be confirmed, and Senator Griffin of Michigan, with great want of enthusiasm, predicted that the "appointment will be confirmed with my support."[7] On September 24, before the opponents testified, Senator Bayh predicted that Haynsworth would be confirmed. Columnist James Kilpatrick reported that antisouthern sentiment was gathering; that the objection was that Haynsworth was "a moderately conservative Southerner. That is enough. Lynch him!"[8] The main opposition had surfaced, but *U.S. News and World Report* on September 15 predicted that Haynsworth would win confirmation. On September 24 Eastland told Walters that "labor is all out to defeat nomination." A poll on that day recorded twenty-five senators as against Haynsworth, but Eastland felt that that figure was too low. By September 25 Eastland was worried. He noted with reference to Senator Charles Mathias of Maryland, "more and more looks like he's lost. A love feast between him and Rauh." Eastland did not know how Senator Tom Dodd of Connecticut would vote.[9]

On September 16 the committee was called to order, briefly mourned for Dirksen, and turned to the appointment. Senators Thurmond and Hollings of South Carolina presented the judge to the committee. Hollings, who knew Haynsworth well, took full credit for having originally suggested the appointment. He also took a vigorous slash at the critics: "Now, as a senator, I find that in presenting him, I must defend him. I do so with pride, because I first suggested him to President Nixon last May. But this is not totally accurate. Actually, the Judge's record of achievement has been suggesting him for the highest judgeship for some time, and to the President's credit, he was the first to recognize it." Hollings continued, "Of course there is no conflict of interest." He cited cases for the proposition that a judge must disqualify himself when he should, but that, on the other hand, "it is equally his duty to sit when there is no valid reason" not to.[10]

The hearings on the first day were directed essentially to *Vend-a-Matic,* with Haynsworth the lead witness for a day and a half and the ABA witness and I on the second and third days of the hearings. Charles Wright and others were never called by virtue of a decision of Chairman Eastland that it was politically more necessary to get done than to enlarge the record even with important material.

The committee wanted to hear about *Vend-a-Matic,* and Judge Haynsworth obliged instantly at the hearing. As early as September 6 Hollings reported that some senators thought that Haynsworth should not have sat in the *Darlington* case. The first question asked by Chairman Eastland was whether Haynsworth had ever heard of *Vend-a-Matic,* and he responded, doubtless a little ruefully, "I have heard a great deal of it, yes, sir."[11] He described the growth of the Vend-a-Matic vending machine company created by the members of his own law firm plus a business friend. At first the machines dispensed coffee, and then foods, candy, and a miscellany of edible items were added. Deering-Milliken had some twenty-seven mills in the Southeast, and when Haynsworth became a circuit judge in 1957, Vend-a-Matic machines were in two of those mills. It lost one in 1958. In 1963, when the *Darlington* case came before the court, Vend-a-Matic bid against seven competitors as to one Deering-Milliken mill and won it, and it bid for two others and lost. Of the 19,000 Deering-Milliken employees, Vend-a-Matic did business with about 700.

The gross business with the 700 employees was about $100,000, which amounted to about 3 percent of Vend-a-Matic's total business. Deering-Milliken did no favors for Vend-a-Matic, and the man who let the contract gave evidence that he had never heard of Haynsworth. When Haynsworth went to the circuit court, he was a director of several companies. He dropped out of all but two, one an extremely small and local affair and the other Vend-a-Matic. But in 1963 the Judicial Conference of the United States recommended that judges disassociate themselves altogether from such positions, and he then resigned from those two.[12]

Senator McClellan of Arkansas pointed out that Vend-a-Matic not merely had no litigation before Judge Haynsworth, it never had any litigation of any kind. After a desultory interlude, Senator Sam Ervin of North

Carolina began his turn with a tribute to Haynsworth: "I have reached the honest and abiding conviction from reading your opinions that you have discharged your duties as a member of the U.S. Court of Appeals for the Fourth Circuit with what Edmund Burke called 'the cold neutrality of the impartial judge.' I know of no higher tribute that can be paid to any occupant of a judicial office." [13] The dialogue went into the details of the *Darlington* case—what was decided, how had Judge Haynsworth voted on this or that detail, and so on. After the first day's testimony, the *Columbia Record* of September 17 reported that the judge "appeared edgy and stuttering under hours of questioning" but declared that he had never decided a case in which he had had a financial interest.

The fourth circuit is a small circuit (Maryland, Virginia, West Virginia, North Carolina, and South Carolina), but by chance it had four members on the Judiciary Committee, senators Ervin, Thurmond, Tydings, and Robert Byrd of West Virginia. Because of an almost family quality of the bar of the fourth circuit, these senators had a special feeling of knowing their judges, and Senator Tydings, early to question Haynsworth, was very much of that family. As a U.S. attorney, he had often appeared before Judge Haynsworth, and as chairman of a subcommittee of the Judiciary Committee having to do with courts, he had dealt especially with Haynsworth. He reported to his colleagues that as a lawyer of the fourth circuit, he found Judge Haynsworth to be "thoughtful, fair and open minded" and as a court administrator, "innovative and, indeed, dynamic." Tydings briefly discussed Haynsworth's opinions, some of which he agreed with and some of which he did not, only to declare that in his view this was irrelevant; the test for confirmation of a judge should not be whether one agrees with his conclusions but whether he has "demonstrated a proper judicial temperament, an intellectual capacity equal to the tasks set for him, and a character beyond reproach." [14]

Tydings turned to Vend-a-Matic. In response to questions, Haynsworth identified his original investment in Vend-a-Matic, explained that he endorsed notes that ran up to several hundred thousand dollars to cover bank loans, and stated that he met from time to time with the board of directors. He never in any way solicited any business from Deering-Milliken. His highest annual return in director's fees was $2,600. When the company was sold, the purchaser took the stock but not all of the land that belonged to Vend-a-Matic. This came back to some of the original owners and was then leased to the purchasing company; Haynsworth's interest in the real estate was about $9,000, engendering a few hundred dollars a year in income.[15]

As for Haynsworth's connections with Deering-Milliken while in the practice, he had for a long time represented a local mill in Greenville which provided considerable legal work to his office. When this mill was acquired by Deering-Milliken, the Haynsworth office lost most of the business. When the *Darlington* case came before his court, Judge Haynsworth did not consider disqualifying himself; the possibility never occurred to him. At the time he was not consciously aware of any connection he had.

Judge Haynsworth had replied to the letter from senators Hart and Tydings on September 6. He included a list of forty-six plants in which Vend-a-Matic had full-service food distribution in 1963. It never had any machines in the Darlington Manufacturing Company plant that was the immediate subject of the lawsuit. Even so, he laid it on the line that while he had not known where the particular machines were, if he had known he would not have disqualified himself, for he had a duty to sit where, as he believed, there was no legal disqualification. He noted the disruptive effects of disqualifications, particularly in a small circuit, and quoted the very distinguished Alabama circuit judge Richard T. Rives in *Edward v. United States,* who concluded regretfully that "in the absence of a valid legal reason, I have no right to disqualify myself and must sit." [16] His reply also included an extensive account of his other investments.

Up to this point, the hearings had been a love feast. There had been no witness criticism of Haynsworth for anything but merely inquiries into what was being systematically demonstrated to be a dry hole. But at this point Tydings tossed in a small bomb. Judge Haynsworth's predecessor as the presiding judge of the fourth circuit was Judge Simon Sobeloff of Baltimore. Sobeloff had written an article which Tydings quoted: "One can readily see that if a judge serves as an officer or a director of a commercial enterprise, not only is he disqualified in cases involving that enterprise, but his impartiality may also be consciously or unconsciously affected when persons having business relations with his company come before him." Vend-a-Matic had business relations with Deering-Milliken, parent of Darlington. Did this "consciously or unconsciously" affect Judge Haynsworth? [17]

The question put Haynsworth in a box. The fact is a judge having some connection with a supplier of a party is not automatically disqualified. Judge Sobeloff had not said otherwise, but his article was open to a broader construction than, perhaps, he had meant. Haynsworth responded that the only even theoretical influence he could have been subject to was in his capacity as a stockholder, "and this could have resulted in some financial interest if my interest as a stockholder was known and someone doing business with Vend-a-Matic sought to influence my vote to do something I otherwise would not have done."[18] But those assumptions were contrary to the record, and he therefore thought there could be no financial influence. On the other hand, if he held stock in a party, he did disqualify; for example, he held stock in J. P. Stevens, a giant and militantly antilabor textile company, and Haynsworth did not sit in its cases.

Bayh asked whether, if the identical matter rose again, Haynsworth would still choose to sit on the case. Haynsworth replied, "Even if I knew at the time all that I know about it now, I would feel compelled to sit."[19] The hearing then swerved to a general ruckus over just what the clearance in 1964 by Attorney General Kennedy covered. Senators Bayh and Kennedy thought that it covered only the question of bribery, of throwing a contract and that it was this charge which was disproved; senators Eastland and Ervin thought that it covered any claimed conflict of interest as well. The matter was poignant for Senator Kennedy, since his recently assassinated brother was the attorney general involved. Senator Kennedy observed that he too had "complete confidence in Judge Haynsworth."[20] Judge Haynsworth himself was then asked whether he felt that the committee was bound by the 1963–64 investigation. The judge responded:

No. . . .

As far as foreclosing inquiry in the Senate, I do not think so. Indeed the question having been raised, I want the Senate to pass on the merits. And my position is that if a hundred judges and a hundred bishops and everybody else swore in 1964 that I had committed no impropriety whatsoever, the question is before this Senate and I want the judgment of this Senate. I may say that while I am concerned about myself and my reputation, I much more am concerned about my country and the Supreme Court as an institution, and if there is substantial doubt about the propriety of what I did and my fitness to sit on the Supreme Court, then I hope the Senate will resolve the doubt against me.[21]

As always, the conversation returned to the *Darlington* case. The hearing was dragging, and the witnesses began to come by squadrons; five congressmen testified together. The net effect was negative on the civil rights issues, with nothing new being added. The same is true of William Pollock, the general president of the Textile Workers Union, except that Pollock had been peculiarly at the center of the 1963 charges against Haynsworth which had gone to the chief judge of the fourth circuit and the Department of Justice and on which Haynsworth had been completely cleared.

Pollock sought to distinguish between what he claimed was a charge purely of bribery in the first instance and not a charge of conflict of interest. The union's position was that it had no knowledge of Judge Haynsworth's connection with Vend-a-Matic and did not know that the firm which had incorporated a subsidiary of Vend-a-Matic in North Carolina was the same law firm which represented Darlington, the employer. The real union point, as expressed by Pollock, was a belief that "Judge Haynsworth is imbued with the philosophy" of a "conspiracy" among the giant corporations of the southern textile industry "to deny more than a half million American textile workers their right to form and join unions."[22]

Senator Ervin examined the actuality of the asserted ignorance of the witnesses. The union's report to the Justice Department had centered on the charge that on December 17, 1963, Haynsworth was first vice president of Vend-a-Matic and that, while he was not aware of the exact number of shares he held, he had been first vice president since the company was formed. While the *Darlington* case already had been decided by the circuit court of appeals, the case was still pending in the Supreme Court when the charges were made. Senator Ervin's point was that had the union thought Judge Haynsworth was disqualified because of his connection with Vend-a-Matic, it could have made a motion at the Supreme Court level to set aside the decision and to ask for a new hearing due to the asserted interest. This was not done. The conclusion was inescapable that there was only an after-the-fact ambiguity as to the scope of the exculpating letter of Attorney General Kennedy; the claim of disqualification was a 1969 afterthought on the 1963 episode.

Haynsworth had laid his disqualification position on the line by his statement that if the *Darlington* case returned, in the same circumstances, he would regard it as his duty to sit. The Senate responded for the moment by turning to other witnesses. I was the first, appearing at the request of the chairman of the committee as an expert on disqualification. The question presented was whether Judge Haynsworth might properly have disqualified himself in the *Darlington* case.

My explanation started from the fact that there existed within the United States two very different views on disqualification of judges. One was the "soft disqualification" view prevalent particularly in the newer states of the Union, that a judge might casually either disqualify himself or be disqualified; for example, in my own state of Arizona an attorney could disqualify a judge simply for the asking. The opposite, or "hard disqualification," view is that a judge cannot disqualify unless he is squarely within the exact grounds for disqualification; otherwise, he has an absolute "duty to sit" no matter how obnoxious it may be to him to do so. The federal system was a hard disqualification jurisdiction, principally because of the very limited number of federal judges and the awkwardness of finding substitutes. Hence, my testimony: "The federal judge operates in a system in which the cases have uniformly held from the beginning that either he is disqualified in the strict sense or he must sit; and there is not any third possibility." [23]

Before 1948 it was the overwhelming practice among the state and federal judges of the country to disqualify if they had any interest in a party before them. In a national survey made in 1946, twenty-six state supreme courts and seven federal courts of appeal reported that the judges of their courts did disqualify in such cases, although there were a few exceptions; two state and two federal courts reported that the judges did not disqualify where the holding was extremely small, usually after obtaining a waiver from the parties. The fundamental rule was that any interest was disqualifying.

The acts of Congress relating to disqualification are a very minor part of a giant statute, the Federal Judicial Code. A standard desk copy of that code runs to 330 pages, and the disqualification provision relevant here is about three-quarters of one page; in 1969, before the statutory revisions that followed the Haynsworth experience, the disqualifications provision was only a few lines.

From time to time the Federal Judicial Code is rewritten simply because it becomes clumsy, obsolete, or disorganized as supplemental statutes are passed which may not fit in very well. Such a revision of the entire Judicial Code occurred in 1948. Before the 1948 codification, the relevant provision was that a federal judge would disqualify if he had "an interest" in the matter. In 1948, as an extremely minor incident of the general revision of this booklike statute, the word "substantial" was inserted before the word "interest" so that the law as it existed throughout Judge Haynsworth's tenure up to the time of his Supreme Court nomination was that a judge should be disqualified if he had "a substantial interest" in a case. No history explains the change.

After 1948 some judges did begin to sit in cases involving corporations in which they had very small holdings; it was customary to seek waivers of the parties in some of those cases but not all.[24] Judge Harrison Winter testified that under the fourth circuit practice, minor holdings did not require disqualification.

My testimony applied the rules to the case at hand. According to the 1946 national survey, "the heavy weight of opinion in America is that if the judge had any interest in a corporation which is a party, he may not sit." On the other hand, where the judge had an interest in a nonparty, the rule had been that he was not disqualified. Thus, if a judge had an interest in a supplier of a party, as, for example, a bank in which a party kept its money or from which it made its loans, the judge was not disqualified unless the case involved the particular account or the particular loan. The third party—the bank or, in this case, Vend-a-Matic—must have a direct interest in the particular case in order for the judge to be disqualified. The conclusion was that there was not "a reported case in the United States in which any federal judge has ever disqualified in circumstances in the remotest degree like those here." Continuing, "It is possible that your committee may wish to change the rules of disqualification. It is possible that one of the committees, Senator Bayh's committee or another, may wish to make recommendations for altering" the law.[25] But under the law as it existed in 1963 when Judge Haynsworth heard *Darlington,* he had no choice whatsoever but to sit.

I had identified myself as a legal "liberal" and a strong supporter of the Warren Court. Senator McClellan picked the point up and asked a question to which I responded, referring to Canon 8 of the Canons of Ethics, which gives the bar the duty of defending judges from unjust criticism, and continued:

> Obviously given my point of view and experience I would without doubt have preferred a different administration to be appointing a more liberal Justice. But my side lost an election, and the fact of the matter is that as members of the bar we are called upon by Canon 8 to rise to the defense of judges unjustly criticized; and it is my abiding conviction, sir, that the criticism directed to the disqualification or nondisqualification of Judge Haynsworth is a truly unjust criticism which cannot be fairly made.[26]

Senator Bayh then dropped his blockbuster. He asked me for my views on *Brunswick Corp. v. Long*.[27] As Bayh stated it, Haynsworth had sat in the *Brunswick* case at a time when he owned a thousand shares of Brunswick, worth around $17,500. Acknowledging that I never heard of the *Brunswick* case before, I expressed again the view that a judge should not sit in a case in which he owns stock in a party. Fortunately, the senator was willing to put *Brunswick* aside. Bayh said, "One more go-around on *Darlington* and we will leave it because we have had a go-around and it is worn out." Continuing, Bayh led the discussion back to the federal statute. I replied that if Bayh wished his views to prevail generally, he would need, through the subcommittee of which he was chairman, to amend the federal statute "to modify the duty-to-sit rule."[28]

By September 22 the *Brunswick* story had broken, and the *Washington Post* landed on it. In an editorial, that paper declared that the episode raised "serious questions about [Haynsworth's] sensitivity to the extremely high standards of conduct that are properly expected of any federal judge, particularly a Justice of the Supreme Court." The *Post* argued that this conduct was not dishonest, but that it exhibited an insensitivity to the "appearance of impropriety."[29] *Time* magazine found the *Vend-a-Matic* case well met and largely disposed of by the testimony but found Haynsworth to be in genuine trouble on the *Brunswick* case. After *Brunswick,* said *Time*, "those less committed to his appointment are beginning to waiver."[30]

Darlington was a ready subject for senatorial discussion because it was well known due to the earlier fuss made about it, but *Brunswick* had to be dug out to know that it existed at all. It was the product of the requests that Haynsworth supply details of each of his stock transaction since 1957. Once the senators had the list of stocks, somebody matched the list with the thousand cases on which Haynsworth had sat, and thus the *Brunswick* case was turned up.

All this investigation took an enormous staff for the opposition. Haynsworth, when the hearings opened, had no staff except cousin Harry. Harry Haynsworth got the impression that the opposition senators pooled their staffs and that the particular part of the job of integrating the judge's cases and his investments was done by a very capable lawyer named James Flug on Senator Kennedy's staff. "Afterward," Judge Haynsworth reported, "I said to the chairman that I thought that a nominee in my position should be provided in fairness with a staff equal to the combined staff of two or three members of the Senate." In the Department of Justice, Rehnquist and at least two men working under him were involved; Rehnquist gave Haynsworth intense private grilling or rehearsal to avoid surprises on the stand. Johnnie Walters was indefatigable.[31]

Walters kept close notes on the *Vend-a-Matic* matters and felt that Haynsworth should clarify that he was not aware of all the contracts of the company when he was sitting and only recently learned about these things and that he should explain the circumstances of his stock investment a little more fully. He had other suggestions for Haynsworth: he should speak into the microphone, he should speak slowly and deliberately, he should not hurry, and he should not get angry or excited. Other than his coaching by Rehnquist and Walters, Haynsworth had virtually no contact with what was going on at the Justice Department.[32]

On September 16, during the noon hour, Stephen Schlossberg, general counsel for the United Auto Workers (UAW), sent Bayh a handwritten note reporting the Brunswick episode. Senator Bayh wrote to Eastland on September 19, noting that in discussing the subject of judicial ethics with me during the previous day's session he had "inadvertently raised the question of the Brunswick Corporation case before Judge Haynsworth." He thought that my opinion on the ethical question of stock ownership was important. He regretted that he had been unable to talk to the judge personally and "put it to rest once and for all." "I believe it is extremely important, both to the Judge and to the decision before it, to get the facts necessary to clear the air on this subject." He had asked Senator Hollings to get this information from Judge Haynsworth but did not yet have it. "I am concerned about the various rumors which are rampant" concerning *Brunswick*. If the Senate could not get the necessary documents otherwise, he wanted to subpoena them.[33]

The American Bar Association next reported its views by the testimony of one of its most prestigious members, former federal district judge and deputy U.S. attorney Lawrence E. Walsh, chairman of the relevant ABA committee. The committee found Judge Haynsworth "highly acceptable from the viewpoint of professional qualification." With respect to the *Darlington* case, it found that there had been no conflict of interest and that Judge Haynsworth had a duty to sit as a member of that court. Senator Bayh took Judge Walsh into the *Brunswick* matter, asking whether he held the view that any judge who had stock in a corporation must disqualify himself. Walsh recognized this as the majority view but noted that in the fourth circuit some judges had not disqualified if their holdings were very small.[34]

On September 19 Walters reported to Rehnquist his telephone conversation that day with Judge Harrison Winter of Baltimore, the judge next senior to Haynsworth on the fourth circuit, on the subject of *Brunswick*. Winter was very specific and very firm that never after November 10, 1967, was there any doubt about the decision in the case. Rehnquist utilized this information in a letter to Senator Eastland on *Brunswick*, and Winter came to testify about it.[35]

The matter at issue was whether the Brunswick Corporation, which had furnished the equipment for a bowling alley, or the landlord of the premises should have the first priority in being paid when the bowling alley went broke. The case was argued and decided in conference on November 10, 1967. The panel found it a minor case. Winter wrote the opinion and circulated it to the other two judges, Haynsworth and Woodrow Wilson Jones, on December 27; Judge Jones joined on December 29. Haynsworth joined on January 9, 1968. The opinion became final on February 1.

Meanwhile, Haynsworth had a customary end-of-year meeting on December 15, 1967, in Greenville with Arthur McCall, who managed his investments. The purpose was to consider readjustments in his portfolio for tax or other reasons. In this case, he had recently sold some stock, and McCall recommended that he invest the proceeds in Brunswick. With Haynsworth's approval, McCall bought a thousand shares of the 18 million Brunswick shares outstanding for $16,000 on December 26. Brunswick had had an acute downward fluctuation, and McCall had recommended the purchase in the belief that it would come back. McCall, at the time of this purchase, was recommending Brunswick to his other customers as well; his aggregate Brunswick purchases at the time were about 15,500 shares.[36]

Committee member Senator William B. Spong of Virginia was troubled at the *Brunswick* matter and asked me for a written opinion concerning it. Meanwhile, the giant fifth circuit court of appeals, with its headquarters at New Orleans, issued an opinion and order expressly declaring the right of a judge to sit in a case where his interest was not "substantial." This declaration amounted to an express, though indirect, endorsement of Haynsworth's conduct in the various cases under discussion.[37] There were two fifth circuit cases bearing on disqualification.[38]

In the first case, the trial judge had a hundred out of 36 million shares in the company, worth about $10,000. The fifth circuit held, by vote of all ten judges, that "this tiny fractional interest in the equity ownership of this huge industrial enterprise does not amount, either as a matter of fact, or law, or both, to a substantial interest by the trial judge." I called this opinion to the attention of Senator Spong, who did, in fact, vote for confirmation.

Senator Tydings had another problem. In his capacity as chairman of the Subcommittee on Judicial Improvements, three months earlier, on June 2, he had taken the testimony of Judge Haynsworth on a proposed bill to require disclosure by judges of their financial holdings. He had asked Judge Haynsworth for his views; in the course of his answer, Judge Haynsworth had rambled a little and gratuitously said: "Of course, when I went on the Bench I resigned from all such business associations I had, directorships and things of that sort. The only one I retained is the trustee-ship of this small foundation which I mentioned in my main statement, and I think that perhaps the best rule for a judge to go by now is to stop doing even that much." Tydings now asked, "When you went on the Bench you did not resign from all business associations. You resigned from all except two." Haynsworth agreed but pointed out that by the time he had appeared before Tydings he had resigned from those and had retained only the trusteeship of the small foundation.[39]

Haynsworth had been serving as a judge consulting with the ABA's committee on professional ethics. Tydings noted that the Judicial Conference in 1963 had adopted a resolution that a judge should not serve as an officer, director, or proprietor of an organization formed for profit. Haynsworth again pointed out that once this resolution was adopted, "I promptly accepted what the Conference had done and resigned from these two directorships." Tydings described the very extensive financial reporting he wanted from judges and asked Haynsworth whether he would object. Haynsworth replied that as Tydings knew, he had been supporting the Tydings proposals.[40] As a presiding judge of a circuit, Haynsworth was a member of the Judicial Conference of the United States. He had supported financial disclosure requirements there.

In the course of the hearings at a later point, the judge was asked about his testimony before the Tydings committee in which he said that he had resigned from all corporate directorships when he went on the court in 1957. In 1957 he was a member of the board of nine separate corporations, of which seven had a large number of stockholders. He resigned as director of those seven corporations, including a bank and a life insurance company. The other two were very closely held concerns, one with seven stockholders and one in which three families were involved in which he represented his mother, sister, and brothers. In 1963, after the Judicial Conference vote, he went off the other two, not because he thought it was a particularly useful thing to do, but simply because that was the rule. The testimony before the Tydings committee in 1969 was a casual interjection of his own, and he felt that those two corporations were not within the reason of the rule they were talking about in 1969; as he observed in the confirmation hearing, his statement was true as of the time of the Tydings hearing.[41]

Tydings noted that there had been talk of violation by Haynsworth of Canon 26 of the Code of Judicial Ethics. That canon directs judges not to make personal investments in enterprises apt to be involved in court litigation and, if he has such investments when he becomes a judge, advises him to dispose of them. Haynsworth responded that Vend-a-Matic was not merely not likely to be involved in a lawsuit, it had never been involved in a lawsuit. The canon also provided that the judge should "refrain from all relations which would normally tend to arouse the suspicions that such relations warp or bias his judgment, or prevent his impartial attitude." Haynsworth supposed that this section was directed to "relations with gamblers and people like this, with backgrounds that were suspect or shady. And I have no such relations."[42]

When Tydings got the Darlington Mills papers, he said to Haynsworth, "Oh my God, we'll have to ask you a lot of questions." Haynsworth replied, "All right, Joe, that's perfectly all right with me, please do."[43] That was the last conversation he had with Tydings. Haynsworth was very popular in Maryland, and all five district judges there were strongly for him. However, on the question of what, if anything, was done to marshal sentiment in Maryland for him, Haynsworth had no knowledge. The Baltimore newspapers were very much against him; they were sympathetic to unions. He felt that the fact that Senator Mathias, as a Republican, wound up against him also had strong influence on Tydings because Tydings, as a Democrat running for reelection, could not afford to support him if the Republican senator did not.[44]

V

Interlude

The Outlook of Judge Haynsworth

Just before the hearings started, Lewis Powell, then a leading Richmond attorney, wrote to Senator Tydings:

> Knowing Clement Haynsworth as a man over the years, I have no doubt as to his character and integrity. I have never heard a lawyer or a judge in the Fourth Circuit suggest any racial or labor bias on the part of Judge Haynsworth. A confirmation should not turn on the political classifications of liberal or conservative. A nominee should be judged on the basis of his character, experience, and demonstrated ability as a lawyer and judge. I had little patience with the ultra conservatives who attacked prior nominees on the ground that they were too liberal. I would hope that this example is not followed, in reverse, with respect to Clement Haynsworth.[1]

When Senator Tydings finished, Senator Hart of Michigan began his questioning. Judiciary was a strong committee, and Hart was one of its most respected members. As a demonstration of the attitude of his fellow senators toward him, when he died prematurely of cancer, one of the Senate office buildings was given his name. As a liberal Democrat, he inevitably would not have found Haynsworth to his taste as a possible choice, but at the same time he recognized that it was the prerogative of the president, not the Senate, to make that choice. There had been much talk in the press that Haynsworth was a "strict constructionist." Hart began by asking what the term meant and whether Haynsworth was one. Haynsworth replied: "Senator, I have been said to be one. I don't know— I don't know what it is and I certainly do not know that I am one. Again, one can read what I have written as a judge and draw conclusions from it. But I have not labeled myself a strict constructionist. And I think if you read some opinions I have written, you would not think I was." Hart continued, inquiring whether this term had been discussed with Haynsworth by President Nixon, to which Haynsworth replied that "the term has not been defined to me by anyone." [2]

Hart moved a little closer to the core of things, observing that certainly in the mind of President Nixon, "Earl Warren is not a strict constructionist. That opinion is shared by many. I think he was an outstanding, a magnificent Chief Justice." To which Haynsworth carefully replied, "He is a very close friend of mine." Then came a little colloquy in which the very bright Senator Ervin of North Carolina caught the very bright Senator Hart of Michigan off base. Hart had begun his examination with a comment that he had long insisted that it was undesirable to cross-examine judges on specific cases. He now proceeded to do just that. Taking off from his question on Chief Justice Warren, Hart continued that Warren had "got into trouble" because he had held that "separate but equal wasn't equal and wasn't constitutional." He asked Haynsworth whether he agreed with Warren in that regard, and Haynsworth replied, "I certainly do," thus flatly affirming his own view that segregation was unconstitutional. Hart dug a little further; referring to the opinion of the Warren Court that all persons were entitled to counsel in criminal cases, he asked Haynsworth, "Now, do you think that is good?" to which Haynsworth replied, "Senator, we have upheld that right again and again in my court." [3]

At this point, Senator Ervin pounced. Jibing Hart, he observed, "I am glad at long last the senator from Michigan agrees with me that a senator has a right to ascertain the views of a nominee of the Supreme Court." To which Hart responded weakly, "I am ascertaining whether he agrees with Earl Warren." Ervin, a bit smugly, observed that when in the past he had attempted to ask questions as to the legal points of view of judges, "I was told at the time that it was highly improper for me to seek to ascertain" such opinions. [4]

Senator Hart then backed off his coyness. He wished to find out "if we were asked to consent to the nomination of a man who thought that the direction of the Supreme Court under Earl Warren should be reversed or modified. Now, I think that it is a fair question because on its answer hinges, I suspect, my vote." Haynsworth replied with dignity that he believed that he should not speculate on what he would do in particular cases which might come before him as a justice, but that he felt that his own writings in the many years he had been a circuit judge would give Hart all of the answers he needed on these points and that there would be other witnesses to expound on those opinions.[5]

Hart put into the record a table of opinions by Haynsworth which, though he did not say so, were obviously selected because they gave him some unease. He said:

> We don't have to be Ph.D.'s in sociology to know that there is great alienation and hostility in the country. It is not the young alone. It is not the black alone. It is not the poor alone.
>
> It has been my feeling that the direction of the Warren Court has strengthened the responsible leadership in this country which urges that inequities be corrected within the law. Slowing down the direction of the Warren Court assists only the irresponsible voices. That's my concern.[6]

Senator Kennedy pursued the topic. What he wished to discuss with Haynsworth was "the frustration and the alienation of the young people," and he asked Haynsworth to express his own views on what he thought were the root causes of the frustration of youth and minority groups. Haynsworth responded that many young people believed "that this country does not realize the promise it held for them when the Constitution was adopted" and that "they are impatient to achieve realization of what they think ought to be the objective of our society."[7] The exchange was inconclusive. Neither the senator nor the judge, for whatever reasons, wished to become explicit about the great pressures caused by the Vietnam War and the dragging pace of desegregation; in consequence, the senator did not clinch his question nor the judge his answer, and the inquiry passed to the main Haynsworth opponent, Senator Birch Bayh of Indiana.

VI

The Attack

Senator Bayh began gently. He suggested that in light of the background of the Fortas retirement there was a special need to assure that the justices were "beyond reproach." This, he thought, put the Haynsworth nomination "in a very special position in history." He added, in a phrase to be important later when all the dust had settled, that the Senate had "an obligation, to set, once and for all, uniform standards and criteria which will be applied specifically to each prospective judicial nominee." Senator Bayh also noted that it was his opinion that Judge Haynsworth was "an honest man, with a fine reputation."[1]

Then Bayh proceeded to what he regarded as the meat of the thing. The first area of questioning was which and how many textile companies did the Haynsworth firm represent, both before and after he went on the bench; there were apparently twenty or so. From the list of companies, the senator moved on to the *Deering-Milliken* case, the dialogue establishing that it was a case of great importance in the field of labor relations.

Bayh then identified his point: he wished to find out about "the relationship that you and your law firm have with the textile industry." Haynsworth left the firm in 1957, and the questioning developed that he had no continuing financial relationship with the firm. A customer-by-customer analysis of Vend-a-Matic followed, demonstrating that perhaps thirty of its customers were textile concerns. Haynsworth's recollection had been that he had resigned as vice president of Vend-a-Matic when he went on the court in 1957, but the company records showed him repeatedly reelected until 1964. This Bayh felt was a "source of some embarrassment" to Haynsworth, while the judge felt it insignificant since he had no duties in the vice-presidential office. The judge's wife continued with very sporadic duties as secretary to Vend-a-Matic, performing services for which in 1962 she was paid $1,500. In this capacity she had signed the minutes that showed the continuing election of Judge Haynsworth, a point of which Senator Bayh made as much as he could.[2]

The questioning then turned to the ABA Canons of Judicial Ethics, and the judge was asked for his practice. He responded that he had complied with the canons and with their spirit. He had not sat in any case in which his former law firm was involved or in any case of another firm in which a cousin of his was involved. He had made no investments in companies likely to be involved with any frequency in his court; he could recall no instance in which he had sat in a case in which he had an investment.

The bête noire of organized labor in the textile industry was the J. P. Stevens Company, in which Judge Haynsworth held 550 shares of stock. Bayh asked whether this was compatible with the canon that forbids personal investments in enterprises apt to be involved in litigation. Haynsworth replied that the suggestion of any impropriety did not fit. There had, in fact, been two or three Stevens cases since he had been on the court, and no more; he did not regard this as "frequent litigation." More solidly in his mind, he would not have sat in the Stevens cases in any instance because Stevens had long been a major client of his office.

Bayh's staff had done its homework. Haynsworth had said that he would not sit in the J. P. Stevens matters because of his firm's close relationship with the company. Bayh then turned to a whole series of other cases in which firm clients had been before the court, thus forcing a colloquy as to whether they were more or less close to the firm than J. P. Stevens. But Haynsworth had sat in no cases in which his firm was involved, and Bayh dropped the subject.[3]

An unfortunate episode from the Haynsworth standpoint was the confusion over the order of calling witnesses that precluded the appearance by Roy Wilkins, the head of the NAACP, who was going to Europe. The leading opposition attorney made a great scene; Harry Haynsworth felt that this was a systematic effort to steal the news headlines for the next day and obliterate the favorable tone of the judge's testimony by changing the subject. Haynsworth, however, had nothing to do with the scheduling of witnesses. He was aware that the opposition consistently and adroitly made moves with the next day's headlines in mind. When Eastland cut off the hearings without including all the favorable witnesses, it was because

Eastland thought he had the votes and wanted to get to the floor. That was his decision; Haynsworth, realizing completely that Eastland's political judgment was better than his, nonetheless always regretted that decision. He thought professors Wright and Foster, both omitted in Eastland's rush to judgment, would have given him a good press.[4]

On September 20 Haynsworth responded to a note from Chief Justice Burger sent from Portugal. "In the matter of my induction, I intend to be guided entirely by you. I would be tremendously honored to have you administer the oath to me in open court, but if any other arrangement seems more appropriate to you at the time, I would quite willingly adapt myself to it." He reported that since Burger had written, "It has now become apparent that there is determined opposition to my appointment, and that the opponents on the committee are doing all within their power to prolong and drag out the hearings." The "pace of the proceedings seems to be largely in the control of Senators Hart, Kennedy and Bayh."[5]

It is against that background that Judge Haynsworth took the stand for the last time in his confirmation hearings to answer questions concerning the *Brunswick* case. The matter opened with a broad invitation from the chairman to the judge: "Judge, tell us what you know about this Brunswick stock."[6] Haynsworth reported that the case had been heard and decided on November 10, 1967, and assigned to Judge Winter to write. It had been a rather "fruitless appeal," and the panel considered disposing of it on a brief order that very day; but there was some language in the opinion of the district court under review which they thought should not be affirmed so the written opinion was decided upon.

Senator McClellan thought it important—"most important"—to determine whether the judge had in mind obtaining Brunswick stock when the case came before him. The answer was no—the purchase had been entirely at the later suggestion of his broker. Six weeks after the court's decision he did authorize the purchase of the Brunswick stock. As he said: "The case that we had, of course, did not enter my mind at the time. If it had been in my mind, I would not have bought the stock. I did not check the cases that had been heard in my court and were not disposed of. I think I should have in the course of buying the stock. Afterwards, this is a precaution I would take. I did not take advantage of it then and, of course, I am very sorry I did not."[7]

The next time the case entered his mind was in January when he received the proposed opinion from Judge Winter. At that stage, he realized that the case had not been completely disposed of and he did recall that he had become a stockholder. He concluded that he would endorse the opinion since Judge Winter had written it precisely as had been agreed before he ever purchased the stock. He realized that if he disqualified himself at this stage he might have to disqualify the whole panel and have the entire case re-presented since he had discussed it with the others; in the interest of plain efficiency, he thought it best to live with the mistake and get it over with. He did not justify his action on the ground that the interest he had obtained was not "substantial," although in the opinion of many judges this would have been a reasonable view. Rather, his position was that he would not have bought the stock in the first place had he been aware that there was a case still outstanding relating to that company; this was simply an oversight.[8]

So that there would be no more surprises, Judge Haynsworth obviously had primed the chairman to ask him about his holdings in the Chesapeake and Ohio Railroad. The chairman said jocularly, "I hear you are a big stockholder in the C&O Railroad." He asked the judge to tell them about it.[9] The fact developed that the judge's wife had purchased ten shares for $641 in the C&O to put the Haynsworths in line for one of the shareholders meetings of that railroad which were occasionally held at the Greenbrier, a great resort in West Virginia. Such meetings were attended at the shareholders' expense, and Mrs. Haynsworth was trying to get her husband to take a little holiday. While his wife held this stock, the judge did sit on a C&O case which his court decided against the C&O.

The friendly questions ended. Senator Hart clearly believed that it was a violation of the Canons of Ethics to hold—and to continue to hold, as Haynsworth did—stock in Brunswick since Brunswick appeared apt to be involved in litigation. Judge Haynsworth could give as well as take, and with style. When Senator Bayh went into a series of hostile questions presented in a friendly way, at one point this colloquy occurred:

> Senator Bayh. I was trying to be on your side on this point, Judge.
> Judge Haynsworth. All right. I did not get that notion, but if you are I will be delighted.[10]

Senator Bayh brought the matter back to Vend-a-Matic:

> Senator Bayh. I am concerned and I suppose I should ask the question, if you had to do it over again whether you would still maintain that kind of

relationship with Carolina Vend-a-Matic. You feel that there is absolutely nothing that was improper here?

Judge Haynsworth. I do not know what you mean by that kind of relationship. I was a stockholder as I have said.

Senator Bayh. Stockholder, vice president, and your wife is secretary and you are on the board of directors and you own $450,000 worth of stock. You were doing business with one of the litigants.[11]

The *Vend-a-Matic* and *Brunswick* situations were very different. In *Vend-a-Matic*, Haynsworth had stock in a company which did business with a party; until this hearing, no one had supposed that having stock in a supplier of a party was a disqualification unless, in some fashion, the supplier would be directly affected by the case. The supplier is simply too remote. But in *Brunswick* the holding was of stock, no matter how minor, in a party. To the repeated questions, Haynsworth repeatedly responded that had he been a shareholder in Brunswick when that case was heard, he would have disqualified. Indeed, by now, as he responded to Senator Marlow W. Cook of Kentucky, he wished he had never heard of Brunswick. The most telling comment of all was made by Senator Cook, that if the Bayh standards were applied, "no nominee to the Supreme Court of the United States in the future will ever be able to meet" them. Senator Cook acknowledged that he found the *Brunswick* case much more disturbing than *Vend-a-Matic*. Hence, he had written to what he regarded as "one of the finest lawyers" in Kentucky for advice. That lawyer had replied that a charge of conflict of interest in the *Brunswick* circumstances was "ridiculous" and continued, "any man of intellectual integrity should be ashamed to raise it."[12]

The first two and a half days of hearings had been occupied by both friendly and hostile senators, but all the witnesses were friendly. On the afternoon of September 18, the gloves came off and the opposition began hitting. The first witness was George Meany, president of the AFL-CIO, flanked by Andrew Biemiller, his legislative director, and Thomas E. Harris, his associate general counsel. Meany spoke with characteristic bluntness, urging the Senate to refuse to consent to Haynsworth's appointment on three grounds:

His decisions prove him to be anti-labor.

He has demonstrated indifference to the legitimate aspiration of Negroes.

He has demonstrated a lack of ethical standards, while on the Bench, that disqualify him from consideration for promotion.[13]

On the labor point, Meany offered a staff memorandum. In summary, his charge was a record of insensitivity to the needs of employees and instinctive sympathy with the problems of employers, "including rabidly anti-union ones." Meany asserted that Haynsworth had sat on seven labor management relations cases which had been reviewed by the Supreme Court, that in each instance he "took the anti-labor position," and that in each case he was reversed by a virtually unanimous Court. On civil rights matters, the AFL-CIO associated itself with the civil rights spokesman and did not speak independently.

But what Meany asserted to be the most important charge was that Haynsworth had displayed a disregard for "ethical standards" in the *Darlington* case. Under examination it appeared that of the seven cases reviewed at the Supreme Court (and by another count this number was raised to ten), Judge Haynsworth, in fact, wrote the opinion in only one of them. As for the thirty-seven cases involving labor matters in which Haynsworth cast what could be regarded as a "pro-labor" vote and which did not go to the Supreme Court, the AFL-CIO had no report to make.[14]

Meany said that this was the second time the AFL-CIO had opposed a nomination to the Supreme Court in forty years. The first was the nomination of Judge John J. Parker in 1930. Senator Ervin asked Meany whether Judge Parker, who had also been on the fourth circuit court of appeals, had not after his defeat for the Supreme Court become "one of the most distinguished jurists that North America ever has known." Meany agreed. His counsel, Harris, candidly acknowledged that the opposition to Judge Parker "was unjustified."[15]

The hearings began to drift into a tone of savage acrimony with Harris for the AFL-CIO expressly charging Senator Ervin with making "a false accusation" concerning the unions' presentation. As the labor witnesses moved to wind up, Senator Hart began to be overt in his opposition, clearly regretting the "remarkable difference between the attitude of this nominee and the position of the Warren Court." Harris charged Haynsworth with out-and-out falsehoods in relation to Vend-a-Matic, and Senator Cook quickly demonstrated in return that there were no falsehoods and that Harris was stretching. Senator Ervin added to the record the thirty-seven cases at the fourth circuit in which Haynsworth had ruled in favor of the union position, and Cook charged Harris with stressing the Supreme Court cases only because they were "easier to find." [16]

The hearing was getting to be one of the longest on the books; only the Brandeis hearing of 1916 was markedly longer. The last pro-Haynsworth witnesses testified on September 19 and September 23 and then came three days of opponents. The affirmative witnesses were John Bolt Culbertson, president of the Greenville County Bar Association, and Louis P. Fine, the Virginia Bar Lawyers' Association president as well as a Jewish leader in that state. Culbertson, one of the most colorfully effective witnesses at the hearing, was a civil rights lawyer who had experienced crosses being burned in his own yard; with changing times he had become a bar leader. As a staunch supporter of Hubert Humphrey, the Democratic candidate for president in the 1968 election, he cheerfully acknowledged that if his side had won, Haynsworth would never have been appointed. However, as he said, "they won the election, and they have got a right to appoint people with their philosophy, and as long as he is honest, that is the point that I make." Haynsworth he esteemed as "absolutely honest. He has impeccable integrity. He is a man whose word I would believe about anything. I have never put into writing any agreement that I have had with the Haynsworth firm. They are honorable people." As a labor union lawyer, Fine thought it "manifestly unfair to have said that Judge Haynsworth was anti-labor." [17]

Senator Mathias of Maryland asked about a series of civil rights opinions in each of which Judge Haynsworth had been very squarely opposed to discrimination, as when he voted to accelerate integration on a public golf course in his own state or where he voted to void the discriminatory discharge of a black teacher. Clearly Mathias was seeking to demonstrate that any charge of racism by Haynsworth was demonstrably false.

Nineteen witness consumed 250 pages of testimony, all hostile; at that point the chairman thought that it was time to stop talking, and what would have been a dozen other oral statements were put in the record. Congressman William F. Ryan of New York felt that Haynsworth was anti–civil rights. The general counsel of the Industrial Union Department of the AFL-CIO, speaking for that division and for I. W. Abel, head of the United Steelworkers, opposed the appointment and supported Meany's statement. The general counsel for the United Auto Workers was of the same view, as was the general counsel of the International Union of Electrical Workers.

While the attacks to this point had, in some slight degree, touched on civil rights concerns, civil rights had not been at the center of the hearing room stage. On September 25 this changed with the presentation, before a packed hearing room, of Clarence Mitchell, the legislative chairman of the Leadership Conference on Civil Rights, and Joseph L. Rauh, Jr., its counsel. The conference was a group of 125 organizations interested in civil rights; it attacked Culbertson's qualifications to speak for any civil rights groups. On the next day, September 26, eight of the nine black members of the House of Representatives came out in opposition to Haynsworth.

The statement for the group began with the assertion that the nomination of Judge Haynsworth was "a deadly blow at the image of the U.S. Supreme Court" and gained in vigor as it went on. The group saw the blacks of America, with the Haynsworth appointment, becoming lost in "a swamp of delay and technicalities." Judge Haynsworth was not, they said, pressing forward to ensure equality for the black minority; rather he was "for the status quo or for inching along."

Rauh, for the group, presented a detailed argument that on the basis of his opinions Judge Haynsworth was seeking to slow down integration and hang on to segregation, giving a case as an illustration.[18] As he described it, this was a case of a hospital applying for federal aid which expressly declared that it intended to deny admission to some potential patients "because of race, creed, or color." A majority of the court held that the hospital could not discriminate; Judge Haynsworth, as stated by Rauh, dissented on the ground that there was no state action involved in this private hospital and that, hence, it was under no obligation not to discriminate. Rauh claimed that this was directly in conflict with a Supreme Court decision. In a later case, Judge Haynsworth yielded to the majority view in the earlier case but wrote a concurring opinion especially to note that he still thought it wrong.[19] This led Rauh to conclude that Haynsworth was resisting the controlling decisions of the Supreme Court.

The case Rauh regarded as particularly "shocking" was the matter of Prince Edward County.[20] The Supreme Court had invalidated segregation in Prince Edward County, and the county responded by closing all public schools and giving subsidies to parents who would send their children to private schools that were all-white or all-black. Judge Haynsworth, for his court, held the matter pending a determination by the state of Virginia as to the issues involved under the doctrine of abstention. The United States

Supreme Court took the case without waiting for Virginia and ordered the reopening of the schools.

An extensive memorandum on Haynsworth's pro–civil rights decisions was put into the record, distinguishing the Prince Edward County case because it was an abstention matter and listing many cases in which Haynsworth had been very clearly on the pro–civil rights side.[21] The position of the Rauh group was that Haynsworth was giving "us our rights with an eyedropper" because these cases were so clear that they were inevitable.[22] In this dialogue, Senator Ervin of North Carolina was a staunch Haynsworth supporter, and the hearing really became a debate between the Rauh group and Ervin.

All of these details obscured the real war: the basic question was whether the Constitution affirmatively required desegregation, or whether it was enough to permit freedom of choice. The critical fourth circuit case was reversed by the Supreme Court.[23] In that case, Judge Haynsworth, following an earlier fourth circuit decision, upheld a freedom-of-choice plan whereby both black and white students should have complete freedom in choosing which schools they wished to attend. He held that the Constitution forbids discrimination but does not require integration. The Supreme Court, in reversing, held that a freedom-of-choice plan is constitutionally valid only if it promises to eliminate the dual nature of a school system. Since *Bowman,* that issue has been a constant source of tension in some parts of the country; busing is the corollary of the view that desegregation is affirmatively required. By way of simple description, Judge Haynsworth clearly was not in the civil rights vanguard on this issue; he was, equally clearly, in accord with the law of his own circuit, and when he wrote on the subject the Supreme Court had not yet spoken.

Rauh's position was that Judge Haynsworth was not an "admitted segregationist," as was, for illustration, District Judge William H. Cox of Mississippi, a segregation extremist. Rauh's contention was that Haynsworth was no Cox but rather a sort of "laundered segregationist." Senator Hart put a related view: he believed that his colleagues Senator Thurmond of South Carolina and Senator Ervin of North Carolina would be wholly in agreement with Haynsworth's views on desegregation. Senator Hart's concern about "this fellow" was that "he was moving slowly" in civil rights cases.[24]

There followed a group of witnesses, principally black national or regional leaders, who elaborated the civil rights theme. These included the head of the NAACP in Richmond and a Republican district chairman from Detroit important because of such influence as he may have had with Senator Griffin of Michigan, the Republican assistant floor leader. The central thesis was similar to that of the Rauh group.

By this time delays in the hearings had caused many potential witnesses on either side to leave Washington, and in any case, the hearings were far too long already. Prepared statements of some of those witnesses were put in the record, important because they could be used for reports and debate as the nomination moved along. An opposition statement by the Council of the United Church of Christ, a body of some 7,000 local churches with 2 million members, stressed *Vend-a-Matic, Brunswick,* and the ten shares in the C&O Railroad as well as civil rights questions. Other opponents were the National Lawyers Guild, a liberal bar group; an association of the black attorneys in Virginia; and a second association of black attorneys of the southeastern region, as well as two more labor groups.

Filed statements in support came from three very distinguished professors of law. Professor Wright of the University of Texas law faculty, one of the principal constitutional law and procedural law experts in the country, gave a very precise description of Haynsworth's work as neither "conservative" nor "liberal": "The most striking impression one gets from his writing is of a highly disciplined attempt to apply the law as he understands it, rather than to yield to his own policy preferences." [25] His statement as a whole was a scholarly analysis both of the work and of the style of the judge.

A statement by law professor G. W. Foster, Jr., of the University of Wisconsin was particularly useful because Foster, a liberal Democrat, had been very active in the civil rights movement and as a staffer was largely responsible for the Department of Health, Education, and Welfare school desegregation guidelines of 1965. Foster was a figure of both knowledge and eloquence, and it was a hard blow to the Haynsworth cause that he could not be heard from the witness stand. Foster was no apologist for the judge; he did think that some of his opinions were wrong. Nonetheless, the criticisms, he thought, were "gross overstatements." He summed up a detailed analysis:

> Judge Haynsworth is an intelligent, sensitive, reasoning man. He does not fit among that small handful of front-running federal judges who have con-

sistently made new law in the racial area. He has earned a place, however, among those who serve in the best tradition of the system as pragmatic, open-minded men, neither dogmatic nor doctrinaire. His decisions, including those in the racial area, have been consistent with those of other sensitive and thoughtful judges who faced the same problems at the same time. And it simply cannot be said that his record in the racial field marks him as out of step with the directions of the Warren Court.[26]

More tersely, law professor William Van Alstyne of Duke University, a foremost figure in the country on the civil rights matters, concluded that while Judge Haynsworth would not be a "liberal" justice, he would be "an able and conscientious man who will approach his duties on the Supreme Court with a spirit of openmindedness."[27]

The *Columbia State* reported that Haynsworth would be confirmed and that he was being strongly backed by both the president and Attorney General Mitchell.[28] As of September 29, *U.S. News and World Report* was still predicting that Haynsworth would be confirmed. On the other hand, by early October, doubts were widespread. In the *Wall Street Journal* of October 9, Nixon's Haynsworth campaign was seen as a big political gamble. Senator Bayh, seeing victory, said the administration would have a terrible fight on its hands if it did not withdraw the nomination. Informal head counts indicated at least forty or more negative votes. The *Journal* reported that Senator Bayh had developed a chart showing the sharp rise in the Vend-a-Matic sales after Haynsworth went to the fourth circuit. This, charged Bayh, "justified the suspicion that the prestige of his office was used to promote his own interests."

The *Washington Post* on October 9 urged withdrawal. On the other hand, an October 6 editorial in the *Washington Evening Star* said: "One hopes Judge Haynsworth exercises greater care in the future. But we do not believe that this record, as it stands now, can justify a vote against confirmation."

VII

Senatorial Slugging Match

On October 10 Senator Hollings, a key sponsor of the appointment, charged the administration with "fumbling the ball." "They dropped the nominee back in August and let him hang there"; but, he said, "the Administration is working now." Hollings termed Bayh's attack as a "gimmick"; he "is running around like he's distressed with all this information he's digging up; why, he's delighted."[1]

The fact was that President Nixon was indeed pushing for Haynsworth. President Nixon said at his news conference on September 26 that "I have also noted the various items that have been brought up during the course of his hearings in the Senate. I still have confidence in Judge Haynsworth's qualifications, in his integrity. I believe the Senate should approve him. I believe it will."[2] On September 30 the president met with Senate Republican leaders. Senator Gordon Allott of Colorado, chairman of the Senate Republican Policy Committee, told the president that the nomination was "highly controversial" and that he would do well to pull off. Senator Hugh Scott, the new Senate Republican leader, urged withdrawal. Griffin, the assistant to Scott, agreed.

On October 2 Professor Wright, who later was to become counsel to President Nixon in the impeachment proceedings, wrote to congratulate the president and to applaud the firmness with which he was backing Judge Haynsworth. He quoted from recent editorials of the *Washington Post* and the *New York Times* that "there is no valid reason on the basis of the present record for the Senate to deny the President his choice." Professor Wright continued, "If I were the president of a labor union or the head of a civil rights group, I would rather have someone other than

Judge Haynsworth nominated. . . . These groups want someone who can be expected to vote their way every time." [3]

On October 4 Nixon reaffirmed that he was behind Haynsworth. By this time Senator Scott was becoming lukewarm; he declared that he would vote to pass the name to the Senate but he felt that the various cases of claimed interest justified "some careful thought." [4]

Nixon then wrote Scott, as Republican floor leader, asking him to push the nomination, and Scott indicated that he would.[5] On the other hand, by October 3 Senator George Aiken, Republican of Vermont, urged the president to withdraw the nomination because there would be at least forty votes against it. Senators Clifford Case of New Jersey and Edward Brooke of Massachusetts, both Republicans, also asked the president to withdraw the nomination, Senator Brooke terming it "embarrassing." As of that day, the vote appeared to be fifty-six for and about forty against.[6] Meanwhile, the Supreme Court convened with only eight justices.

Scott, up for reelection in November in a state with a big labor and black vote, ended up in the negative. Senator William Saxbe of Ohio claimed that one of his constituents told him that he had been offered federal mortgage backing if Saxbe would support the nomination. Without any apparent instigation, several Republican county chairman in Ohio made it very clear that Saxbe would be their enemy if he opposed Haynsworth.

On October 4 the new senator Ralph Smith, who had been chosen to succeed Senator Dirksen from Illinois, announced himself as opposed to confirmation.[7] Senator Smith told the president, "Anybody who is up for election next year can't afford to vote for Haynsworth." [8] The administration responded by giving the senator an example of real hardball politics. Nixon's campaign manager in Illinois announced that he would oppose Smith in the Republican primary for the next full senatorial term. The governor of Illinois went to Washington to persuade Smith, who also had four separate invitations to the White House. The Illinois Republican delegation in the House, led by GOP whip Leslie C. Arends, met in Smith's office and told the senator his decision would cost him important primary support. In the end, Smith came out for Haynsworth.

Senators Charles Percy of Illinois and Len Jordan of Idaho got a deluge of pressure, including many letters from home; Jordan, on the Senate floor, denounced the pressure he received from the administration. Senator Saxbe of Ohio was invited to the White House for breakfast and went to the Justice Department for lunch with the attorney general. The big blow to Haynsworth was the announcement by Senator John Sherman Cooper of Kentucky that he would vote no, but Senator William Fulbright of Arkansas, expected to vote no, called labor leaders in his home state and asked to be released from that commitment. "The pressure is just too great," he is reported to have said.

The president declared that he was in for the fight. He derided the Brunswick matter as a "cheap, five-dollar affair" and asserted that the rest of the charges were without merit. Later he told the press that he regarded the attack on Haynsworth as "vicious character assassination."

Nixon spent much time in private consultation with individual senators. To Senator Richard Schweiker of Pennsylvania he said, "I do want you to know that I'm really interested, personally, in this one." Others in the administration used more strenuous means. The Republican state chairman in Pennsylvania declared that he was offered a federal district judgeship for one of his own allies if he would get the Pennsylvania senators behind Haynsworth. There were general denials that this conversation took place in just this fashion, but the subject was at least discussed.

Haynsworth was being attacked privately as well as at the hearings. The Justice Department reported a story circulating that Haynsworth "was in partnership" with Bobby Baker, former assistant to the Senate and to President Johnson; Baker had been convicted of larceny and tax evasion in 1967. Haynsworth and Baker had participated in a cemetery investment in 1958 without either knowing that the other was involved, but the name association was enough. All the details of the Baker matter were put into the files. There were two groups of investors in the cemetery, one group from Greenville and the other from Pickens, a nearby town in South Carolina. Haynsworth was a member of the Greenville group to the extent of $4,000; Baker, who was originally from Pickens, was of the other group. It was not until the published reports in 1969 that Haynsworth ever learned of Baker having made a similar investment in the cemetery.[9]

On October 7 Senator Williams of Delaware took up the talk of some relationship between Bobby Baker and Haynsworth which would cast a doubt on Haynsworth.[10] It was singularly appropriate that Senator Williams do this because it was he in 1963 who took the lead in exposing Baker's questionable financial transactions and sent the information to the Justice Department that led to his conviction. Williams told the Senate that he had reviewed his files and could find no reference which would connect Haynsworth with Baker in an improper manner. He strongly urged his colleagues to avoid guilt by association.

In an effort to staunch the flow of support away from Haynsworth, Senator Hollings sent a letter to his colleagues on October 8.[11] That the letter was vintage Hollings was apparent from its first sentence: "My only plea is that the most deliberate body deliberate." He feared that many of the senators were taking positions on the basis of headlines and rumors. Of the 1948 statute on "substantial interest," he said: "We have enacted under present day ethical standards a suspicious standard, which, when adhered to, makes the judge look suspicious. The result is that the judge does as we mandate, and then we fault him for it." He was very concrete: "The *Grace Lines* case is a typical example, which some senators have said to me is the straw that broke the camel's back. The fact is that they do not realize it was a fifty dollar case and they do not realize that today under the statute and canons of ethics it would be the judge's duty to sit."[12]

The October 10 *Time*, as its feature story, reported the seven days just closed as "Nixon's worst week." The Haynsworth matter was a major misery. An unidentified Republican leader was quoted as declaring that the nomination "was a mistake in the first place" and "it's a mistake not to withdraw it." He continued, "It will not help the Republican Party." The nomination had turned out more than the leadership had "bargained for." The attacks on Haynsworth seemed to have been surmounted during the initial weeks of hearing but "then a fresh round of G.O.P. grumblings on Capitol Hill signaled that rancor was turning into revolt. Faced with insurgence, which if combined with Democratic votes could lead eventually to defeat of the Haynsworth nomination, Richard Nixon dug in his heels."[13]

A poll taken by UPI showed thirty-eight senators no, thirty-three yes, and twenty-nine uncommitted. By this time the Nixon administration, fighting for Haynsworth, was using Vice President Spiro T. Agnew as a regular spokesman. On October 15 President Nixon commended Senator Cook, Republican of Kentucky, for pointing out flaws in Senator Bayh's attack. The Cook position was believed by many to be a turning point in favor of the nomination. The American Trial Lawyers Association (ATLA) opposed the nomination, and Senator Hollings, a member and normally a very close friend of that group, criticized the association.[14] Senators Hruska of Nebraska and Cook, both members of the committee, sent a memorandum to the other senators declaring that Haynsworth had a proven record of high standards, that the mere making of accusations was not enough to detract from his high character. Agnew described the various attacks as "character assassination" and the references to Bobby Baker as "whimsical,"[15] but large-scale defections were developing. Of the four Republican leaders, two, Senator Griffin as assistant floor leader and Margaret Chase Smith as chairman of the Republican Conference, came out against.

Time reported that what had brought about the adverse movement was the disclosure of the tenuous business connection with Baker. Investigators querying to Baker received the amused response, "Do you want to ruin my reputation by associating me with Haynsworth?" As *Time* reported, "The real estate deal was apparently innocuous and innocent, but Baker's name is enough to frighten most politicians."[16]

The flood of opposition mail became general, beyond that sponsored by labor and the NAACP. Arizona's Senator Barry Goldwater said: "I had no qualms about Haynsworth at all until I saw a stack of mail on my desk. The usual left-wing mail, you can identify. But it's another matter when you get mail from strict constitutionalists who write, 'Isn't there somebody else?' "[17] There was widespread suspicion that the appointment was the product of a deal between the president and Senator Thurmond of South Carolina to deliver southern votes that would defeat the candidacy of Ronald Reagan in 1972.

By October 11 the nomination was being referred to as the "Haynsworth case." A memorandum by Clark Mollenhoff, deputy counsel to the president who had been an investigative reporter and holder of a Pulitzer Prize, used that title in reporting on the opposition. Johnnie Walters kept a running tally on what could be expected of the various senators; on October 13 he had a comforting estimate of forty-seven yes and twenty-five no, the rest presumably undecided. But his tally for the day before showed forty-two yes and forty-six no with twelve undecided.[18]

The loose cannon on the Haynsworth side was Mollenhoff. Mollenhoff sought and received permission of the Republican State Chairmen's advisory committee to present a summation of the Haynsworth affair before its October 20 meeting in Washington. The chairman warned Mollenhoff not to request passage of a resolution since the committee preferred to hold itself strictly to policy matters. Mollenhoff nonetheless did ask for such a resolution, which was ruled out of order and led to a newspaper's headline, "Haynsworth Rebuffed." Mollenhoff prepared excellent written analyses, but "he gave the appearance of a man gone berserk on a television show, charging his questioners with 'despicable fraud.'" The incident gave rise to a Washington gag about "the Mollenhoff cocktail—you throw it and it backfires."[19]

The tallies drifted toward defeat. By October 20 the UPI showed thirty-six yes, forty-two no, and twenty-two undecided. The president called a special news conference to denounce the attacks. On that same day, *Time* reported that there were about fifty-five votes against Haynsworth; it treated the statements of senators Smith of Maine and Griffin of Michigan as the conclusive developments. Haynsworth was even inaccurately rumored to be considering withdrawal. With singular aptness, *Newsweek* observed: "While most of the public debate over Haynsworth focused on his ethical conduct, it was the prospect of having an essentially conservative Justice on the bench (one whose record on civil rights was moderate at best, and whose decisions in labor cases seemed to have come down consistently on the side of management) that had galvanized these forces into action against him in the first place."[20]

Senator Goldwater followed up his earlier commentary by calling the president. He said: "Mr. President, I am getting telephone calls from people in my state who are upset by the Haynsworth nomination. Some of them are so conservative they think I am a Socialist. They want me to ask you to withdraw the nomination. Look, I'm glad to have a strict constructionist on the Court, but why must we be embarrassed?" However, Goldwater reported that "the President is not to be moved."[21]

Senator Hollings continued to persuade whomever he could; Senator William Proxmire of Wisconsin was one on whom Hollings was working. Hollings did persuade Senator Mike Gravel of Alaska to support Haynsworth, and this decision also persuaded Senator Ted Stevens of that state. One of Walters's notes reports Senator Tydings of Maryland saying that if Mathias would support the nomination, so would Tydings. There were nine other Republicans to be worked on as well. At about the same time, an informant stopped by the Justice Department to talk to Walters and told him that Senator Jordan of Idaho was going to vote against the nomination and "things are getting dangerous." Walters's notes show him deeply involved senator by senator in seeking votes.

The ABA committee on the federal judiciary announced that it was reconsidering its decision. That committee, taking a second look at its endorsement, this time came out with an eight-to-four favorable verdict, a conclusion which *Newsweek* described as pro-Haynsworth but one that damned with faint praise.[22] By this time, even Senator Hollings felt that they were looking at a defeat. Bayh announced that he believed that he had the votes to stop the nomination.

On September 26 the hearings closed; the number of pages with appendices were 762. By way of comparison, three other hearings of that period were on Chief Justice Burger (116 pages); Judge Carswell (465 pages); and Justice Blackmun (134 pages). By November 12 the report of the Judiciary Committee was ready. Ten senators voted to report the nomination with the endorsement that "Judge Haynsworth is extraordinarily well qualified for the post to which he had been nominated." Six senators voted to oppose for a medley of reasons. Senator Scott, Republican floor leader, voted to report the nomination to the Senate on the ground that the final decision should be made by the full Senate; but he took no position on the merits. Senator Griffin, the assistant Republican floor leader, was all-out in opposition.

On November 12 the majority report was presented to the full Senate by Senator Hruska of Nebraska, the ranking Republican on the committee. At the moment, the senator was still confident of confirmation.[23] The committee majority was equally divided between the parties.[24] The report recited the endorsement of the ABA. All six of Haynsworth's colleagues on the fourth circuit court of appeals, including Simon E. Sobeloff, the very liberal presiding judge, had expressed their complete confidence in Haynsworth's integrity and ability, and the majority quoted these expressions.

The majority then turned to the various charges against Judge Haynsworth, clustering these into three categories: first, the claim that he should have disqualified himself in several cases; second, the claim that he should have sold the stock which he owned in J. P. Stevens Company; and third, that he testified untruthfully before the Tydings subcommittee when he appeared before that committee on June 2.

On the *Vend-a-Matic* matter, the committee analyzed the testimony and concluded that the disqualification argument was "contrary to all of the decided cases involving judicial disqualification." It concluded that Haynsworth's sitting in the *Darlington* case "was not merely proper, but was required by law." Additionally, Haynsworth had sat in three cases in which he owned a small amount of stock in a corporation which in turn owned a subsidiary which was involved in litigation. The holdings were, in all cases, minute; in one instance he held 300 shares of stock in a parent company out of 18,252,335 shares. If the term "substantial" in the disqualification statute was given any weight at all, then none of the Haynsworth holdings were even remotely close to substantial. The committee disposed of these on the grounds that the purchase had been inadvertent and the interest was not "substantial." With regard to the inadvertent purchase, the report observed: "This Committee requires a nominee to be honest, honorable, and sensitive to ethical considerations. It does not require him to be infallible."[25]

As for J. P. Stevens, Judge Haynsworth never sat in a Stevens case, a company in which he owned 550 shares, because of his close relations with it as a former client, and since he had a fixed policy of not sitting in those matters, the committee thought what he did with the stock was immaterial.

With reference to the testimony before the Tydings subcommittee, in which he appeared as a witness on a possible disclosure of financial interest by judges, Haynsworth had endorsed a proposal to require disclosure by judges of the names of any businesses with which they were affiliated during a preceding year. He had observed that when he went to the bench, he had resigned from all such businesses, retaining only a trusteeship with a small foundation. As the committee noted, it would have been more accurate to have said that when he went to the bench in 1957 he resigned from seven business associations and that in 1963 he resigned from two others; one of these was Vend-a-Matic.

The committee regarded the misleading aspect of the statement as completely inadvertent; the Tydings subcommittee was considering only matters of future conduct and this was simply a slightly inaccurate "personal reminiscence." This testimony occurred at a time when Judge Haynsworth had already disclosed to the circuit and to the Department of Justice his corporate office in Vend-a-Matic, so that he had no reason to suppress the fact. In these circumstances, the committee found "not the slightest reason to believe that Judge Haynsworth deliberately misrepresented when he freely volunteered information which was not even asked for by the committee."[26] The committee found in what it described as the mere making of unsubstantiated attacks no reason to withhold confirmation.

Turning to the matter of Haynsworth's philosophy and skill, the committee adopted as its own the testimony of Professor Wright as to Haynsworth's "disciplined attempt to apply the law." His civil rights opinions were analytically described, and the testimony of Professor Foster was quoted and adopted. Two dozen cases in which he appeared to be in a pro–civil rights posture were cited. The same device was used as to the labor cases, where there were three dozen "pro-labor" Haynsworth opinions. The passage from Harris in which he agreed that the attack on Judge Parker of North Carolina some forty years earlier had been "unjustified" was included in the report, which analogized Judge Haynsworth to Judge Parker.

The dissents were multiple. Five Democratic senators (Bayh, Burdick, Hart, Kennedy, and Tydings) made a concise joint statement which concluded: "Some of us see flaws in his extra-judicial activities. Some of us have doubts about his record on the appellate bench. And some of us are concerned about his presentations before committees of Congress. But we all share the feeling that our review of the nominee's record leads us to advise the President to withdraw it, and would require us to deny it our consent." [27]

What the five said in an abbreviated fashion, Senator Bayh developed in a fifteen-page expression of his own. Senator Bayh devoted himself entirely to what he regarded as the ethical problems. Acknowledging that Judge Haynsworth was an honest man, Bayh contended he had failed to take "those precautions in his personal and financial relationships which are necessary to avoid even the appearance of impropriety." He made five claims.

First, "on at least four occasions, Judge Haynsworth sat on cases involving corporations in which he had a financial interest and in doing so he violated both the disqualification law and the Canons of Judicial Ethics." [28] The cases were *Brunswick* and the three cases in which he had stock in a company which in turn owned the subsidiary before him. I was quoted at length to the effect that the better view was that any interest should be disqualifying, but with recognition that the word "substantial" in the statute permitted small stockholdings. Senator Bayh presented his authority for the proposition that "the slightest pecuniary interest" should be enough to disqualify. True, said Bayh, the judge bought his stock in the Brunswick Corporation after the case was argued and decided on the purchase without thinking about the case; but he was aware of it when the final acts were taken, and in those circumstances his "failure to disqualify himself or even to notify the parties or his fellow judges of the situation was improper." In this his conduct was not "beyond reproach." [29]

Second, the Canons of Judicial Ethics declared that a judge should avoid investments in "enterprises which are apt to be involved in litigation in the court." Bayh asserted that Haynsworth's various corporate investments were in corporations that were likely to be involved in such litigation.

Third, as to *Vend-a-Matic* and five other cases that involved customers of Vend-a-Matic, Bayh found the judge's participation revealed "insensitivity" and also asserted that these cases violated "the strong precedents of disqualification law and the Canons of Judicial Ethics on this subject." [30]

Fourth, Judge Haynsworth was a trustee of the Vend-a-Matic profit-sharing and retirement plan from 1961 until 1964. A federal statute requires certain reports on such funds, and none were made. Bayh conceded that this was doubtless "an oversight and not an intentional violation" and therefore concluded merely "that complicated financial relationships and judicial responsibility can become a dangerous mixture."

Fifth, Bayh adopted as his own the report of Senator Griffin on matters of candor. He wanted a judge more "sensitive to the many ethical problems which often arise."

Griffin found want of candor in Haynsworth's statements as to just when he had disassociated from Vend-a-Matic, and he criticized Haynsworth's participation in the same cases Bayh had listed. Where Senator Griffin drew blood, in an argument which would echo over and over again, was in the *Grace Lines* case. In *Grace Lines*, an injured seaman claimed $30,000 and was awarded $50. The award was affirmed. Haynsworth owned stock in the parent company of the defendant. Professor David Mellinkoff, at the University of California at Los Angeles, had written to Senator Griffin of this plaintiff: "It is not difficult to imagine the bitterness in the heart of this injured seaman when he learns that one of the judges to whom he appealed in vain, was even a small owner of the company that owns Grace Lines." [31]

Senator Hart refused to concur with the majority on the grounds that the Haynsworth opinions "indicate a consistent insensitivity" to civil rights. Senator Tydings, also quoting the Mellinkoff letter, though in a somewhat different context, joined in objecting on the ground of the judge's participation in the several cases mentioned.

VIII

Campaign and Debate

The focus of the confirmation process is to get the vote, whether for or against, of fifty-one senators. Except as the country's attitude affects those votes, it is immaterial. To the extent that the country's attitude does affect those votes, it is all-important. For the individual senators, the decision is a product of many factors. First and foremost may well be personal conviction. To give two illustrations, the pressures which played across the country had relatively very little effect in either Maine or Kentucky. The two Republican senators from those states divided on the Haynsworth confirmation. Margaret Chase Smith of Maine voted no, and Marlow Cook of Kentucky became a strong supporter. In neither case was there any special persuasion or inducement other than the facts as they saw them.

One of the shrewdest observations in American political history was that of Winfield Scott Hancock, the Democratic candidate for president in 1880, when he said that the tariff was "a local issue." [1] What is commonly accepted as a vast question of international policy is, in fact, at least as much a question of the wishes and needs of the shoe district, the steel district, or, in a more recent decade, the automobile district.

Very much the same can be true of a Supreme Court appointment. Except to the extent that a vote on the nomination becomes a "local issue," it will not make much difference to most senators whether a given nominee is or is not confirmed. With a noncontroversial nomination, there may be no direct political consequence to a senator. The confirmation of Justice Scalia in 1986 probably did not add or detract a single vote from a single senator in the 1986 election.

We deal, then, with a portion of the political process which most of the time is of no political consequence to the individual senator. In Haynsworth's case, intellectual conviction, party loyalty, whether for the president or against him, and regional loyalty were all reflected in votes. For the president there was political advantage to his "Southern strategy." But for the general run of senators, it was the "local issue" that mattered, and both sides played to capture the local interest.

The devices were basically the bludgeon against the rapier, and the bludgeon won. The unions and the civil rights groups could mass very large local pressures, enough to affect elections directly. When Senator Dirksen died and Republican leadership passed to the troika of Scott, Griffin, and Smith, hindsight shows that Haynsworth lost. Both Scott and Griffin faced reelection campaigns in very close states. When Griffin received from the United Auto Workers a resolution such as the following, he could readily see where his own bread was buttered:

> Haynsworth's undistinguished judicial record proves his overt hostility toward workers and their unions and his callous insensitivity to the plight of minorities and all those denied freedom, justice and full civil rights.
>
> Haynsworth is a millionaire judge who, while sitting on the United States Court of Appeals, continued active in a vending machine company doing substantial business with large textile employers, who were parties to cases in the judge's court.
>
> Haynsworth decided cases for corporations in which he held large stock interests; and he did not bother to disclose his interest either to his fellow judges or the parties before his court.[2]

With Bayh as the skillful point man creating a wave of news and with Biemiller and Rauh magnifying the local response to that news, it was immaterial that the end use of the product was exaggerated and distorted, as was this UAW resolution. Griffin got the message, and from similar communications from his own state, so did Scott. They were in positions in which they had everything to gain by a negative vote and nothing of consequence to lose. They had no burning convictions on the matter; after all, the president could be relied upon to nominate some other good appointee. They were in the position of poker players who could casually say to the dealer, "Give me another card."

If the pro-Haynsworth team had had any large groups to use, they would have; but they did not. While the antis could marshal opposition wholesale, the pros could only get support retail, a bit at a time. The central operator in this one-by-one effort was Assistant Attorney General

Johnnie Walters, and he used all of the considerable energy and imagination at his command to get his result. A review of just what was attempted in the last six weeks of the pro-Haynsworth campaign shows how the pro-nomination forces sought votes.[3] For illustration, on October 14 Walters reviewed the activities of Lewis Powell, Haynsworth's strongest supporter in the bar. Powell reported on all five states in the fourth circuit, which at that moment appeared to be 100 percent for the nomination (except for Maryland, this proved to be true). Powell was lining up the former presidents of the ABA to make a united front for Haynsworth, a project which was largely successful. He asked Ross Malone, another former ABA president in New Mexico, to reach Senator Clinton Anderson of that state.

Walters also took up directly with the attorney general what help might be expected from the solicitor general, Erwin Griswold, the figure in the administration most respected at the bar and in the law schools.

Walters took counsel from one adviser, who confirmed what Walters had earlier noted for himself, that Senator Strom Thurmond of South Carolina should not be conspicuous, since Thurmond was widely regarded as the most racist member of the Senate; any support from him would play into the hands of the civil rights opponents. This was no paranoia. The October 1969 *Progressive* wrote that the testimonials of senators Eastland and Thurmond "would suffice, in our view, to cast the gravest doubts on the Haynsworth nomination." It related that the *Chicago Tribune* had reported that Harry Dent, former administrative aide to Senator Thurmond and now Nixon's chief political adviser, conceived of the device of appearing to have Thurmond be for former governor Russell, so that Haynsworth would not seem to be his appointment.

Walters made lists of states with doubtful senators and friendly bar members who could reach them. Many of the calls he made himself. For example, he had the name and office and residence telephone numbers of a Knoxville, Tennessee, lawyer who could speak to Senator Albert Gore of that state, and the note shows, "Okay." This can only mean that the lawyer had agreed to try but not that he achieved the result, since Gore voted no. A former commander of the American Legion could reach a congressman who could reach a senator. Walters speculated as to whether Powell could line up a cadre of retired judges. The next day Powell called back to undertake to try to reach some of the northern former ABA presidents, as for example, Orison Marden of New York, but reported sadly that at least one, and perhaps another, recent ABA president was against Haynsworth.

Walters also kept in close touch with Senator Eastland, a source of forceful suggestions. Eastland suggested that Paul Porter, the former Fortas partner, could persuade Senator Anderson, and Eastland undertook to get a major Texas oil man, also a significant client of Porter's, to give help.

Walters also got the rumors that were afloat, some of them involving his own department and his own adminstration. On October 15 Walters heard gossipy speculation that perhaps the president was setting the nomination up for a fall and that with Senator Scott refusing to say how he would vote, the Haynsworth forces were not getting votes from other Republicans. Walters also was told that his own superior, the attorney general, had consulted some unknown Republicans about the possibility of substituting Judge Henry Friendly of the second circuit for Judge Haynsworth. He received a tip that Senator Aiken of Vermont was suffering from hurt feelings because he had not been consulted by the administration. This slight Walters sought to cure by suggesting that Aiken and his wife be invited to the White House for dinner and, since it was believed that Mrs. Aiken was the strong person in the family, the president speak to her about lining up her husband. Plans were also made to have Senator Harry Byrd, Jr., of Virginia talk to his friend Senator Williams of Delaware, who was reported to be on the fence.

These were intensely busy days. On the fifteenth, John H. Matthews reported on the attitudes of the Nevada senators. Senator Allen Bible had not made up his mind but was receptive and agreed to keep Matthews posted on his thinking. Senator Howard W. Cannon of Nevada was bitter against the president for urging Paul Laxalt, the Republican lieutenant governor of that state, to run for governor. Cannon's complaint was that Nixon in one week asked a strong Republican to run for governor of Cannon's otherwise Democratic state and the next week sent someone to Cannon looking for help on Haynsworth. Walters made special notes of who might get Cannon's more sympathetic ear. He took a call from Salt Lake and discovered that Republican Senator Wallace Bennett was with him but that the Democrat Frank E. Moss would probably go with labor and oppose; someone agreed to talk to Moss.

His reports wrote off senators Frank Church of Idaho and Gale McGee of Wyoming but found questionable senators Leonard Jordan of Idaho and Clifford Hansen of Wyoming, both Republicans. He tabbed some bar leaders to be in touch with Jordan. He got an encouraging word of strong support from Senator Chapman Revercomb of West Virginia, heard an account that Haynsworth might withdraw, and discouraged it. Someone undertook to reach the New Hampshire and Vermont bar presidents. Senator Eastland in the afternoon called back to report that he had been in touch with his friend the Texas capitalist, who had been very good to Senator Anderson of New Mexico on some business deals and undertook to "handle" that matter. Eastland also reported that Senator Jennings Randolph, also of West Virginia, was uncommitted but favorably inclined and made suggestions as to how to nail that down. Eastland also reported that Paul Porter would call Clinton Anderson using Fortas's name and that "if that won't work, nothing will."

Senator Hollings also called, concerned that Judge Haynsworth was "tired and sore" and that the idea was rampant that he might withdraw. Hollings wanted that impression corrected. A good Democrat from Denver called in to report that there was much apathy but that he believed the Colorado senators would support Haynsworth. He believed that California bar support would help in the other western states. A report quoted Ross Malone, former ABA president from New Mexico, who felt that this was a good appointment and that he would talk to Anderson.

October 16 saw another report from Senator Eastland who had talked to Senator Aiken and gotten no impression. Eastland had also spoken to Senator Winston Prouty, the other Republican from Vermont, who was worried because he wanted to support Haynsworth but for political reasons needed to go with Aiken. Paul Porter reported that he could not change Anderson's mind even by invoking Fortas's name. Nonetheless, Eastland believed the supporters should stay on Anderson. Eastland also reported that Jennings Randolph of West Virginia had some close personal connections with certain airline executives, one of whom might be able to persuade Anderson. Another report showed that there was a vacancy for a judgeship on the sixth circuit court of appeals which traditionally had been a Michigan seat. If Griffin was a lost cause on the Haynsworth nomination, then perhaps by switching that appointment to Tennessee and giving it to Senator Gore, that senator might be induced to support Haynsworth.

Other reports showed that the fight had become very vicious as a "backlash from Fortas." Efforts were made to reach Saxbe of Ohio, Aiken of Vermont, the two Pennsylvania senators, and Senator Miller of Iowa. Walters went back to Lewis Powell, from whom he received a detailed report. Powell reported a lengthy conversation the evening before with the president of the ABA, Bernard Segal of Philadelphia. He could not tell whether Segal, a civil rights activist, was for Haynsworth; the most Segal would say was that he had great confidence in the ABA's judiciary committee, which supported Haynsworth, and that the ABA would stand behind him. Powell had also spoken to another former ABA president, Whitney North Seymour of New York.

The next day's report from Pennsylvania reported that Scott was in trouble; it might cost his reelection if he supported Haynsworth. The report was that Scott was in a panic and that anything which could be done to keep him in line would be helpful. Albert Jenner, a prominent Chicago lawyer, called to say that contrary to newspaper reports the final vote of the federal judiciary committee of the ABA had been nine to three in favor and not eight to four. Jenner also reported that his good friend Senator Percy was okay and would stay put; he felt he could "almost guarantee" that result. It was fortunate for Jenner that he did not make the guarantee, because Percy voted no. Jenner also reported that Smith of Illinois did not know what he was going to do but that Jenner had some optimism. An intermediary with another report on Senator Anderson and his staff showed that while Anderson did not want a floor fight on the nomination, in a pinch he would vote no. Walters made a note, perhaps satirical, of a strategy of his own, which was to keep feeding bits of information to Senator Bayh right up to the floor vote; Bayh might then delay the vote to study the information.

Rehnquist reported to Walters that he had talked with Senator Robert W. Packwood of Oregon, who was leaning against confirmation. Packwood had called twenty attorneys in Oregon, and not one of them had asked him to vote to confirm. Walters and Rehnquist agreed to ask Powell to work on the Oregon bar to change that tone. Rehnquist felt that John Kilkenny, recently made United States court of appeals judge from Oregon with the support of both Oregon senators, might be able to persuade Packwood. They agreed that Powell should ask District Judge Walter Craig of Phoenix, another former ABA president, to talk to Kilkenny. Powell did shortly make suggestions about how to deal with Oregon but wanted more help than they were getting from the Republican National Committee. In fact, Richard Kleindienst, the deputy attorney general, called Judge Craig in Phoenix, who talked to Judge Kilkenny. Kilkenny recommended that the department reach four influential lawyers in Oregon, giving their names. Kleindienst reported that the Oregon opposition stemmed from a meeting of the "Bar Association of Portland," poorly attended, at which a negative resolution was passed, which, according to Kleindienst's reports, did not come from the leadership of that bar.

This few days' sample suggests the drive to get the marginal votes. That drive continued to the last minute. Among the many phone calls and maneuvers some high spots stand out. Intense efforts continued to reach the Oregon senators. In addition to the general persuasion, Walters and Eastland agreed that some pending nominations for federal district judges in Oregon, desired by the senators from that state, ought to be postponed until those senators made up their minds about Haynsworth. Numerous lawyers, including one who had been a classmate of the president, were lined up to talk to their senators. Walters talked to Attorney General Mitchell on how to deal with that problem. Possible helpful magazine articles were considered. Someone was found to try to neutralize the American Trial Lawyers Association, which was anti-Haynsworth. Eastland enlisted former senator Earl Clements of Kentucky, whom Eastland regarded as the keenest political mind that had ever been in the Senate; Eastland reported that Clements would help if Hollings asked him to, and Clements did undertake to persuade the railway brotherhoods to get a couple of Senate votes. Senator Hollings worked with Clements on this effort.

Eastland wanted some major lobbyists working on the campaign, particularly Clark Clifford and Edward Bennett Williams. Mitchell liked the idea of involving Clifford and Williams and encouraged Walters to enlist them. Eastland also wanted someone to enlist Tommy Corcoran. Meanwhile, Mitchell was asked to talk to Senator Dodd of Connecticut, who might be weakening in his support; and Powell kept working at his telegram to the ABA presidents. Kleindienst became active in calling Oregon lawyers as Kilkenny had suggested. Hollings went to Europe, and possible negotiations with Senator Ralph Yarborough of Texas were reserved until Hollings, who was Yarborough's good friend, returned. The railway brotherhoods did go to work, seeking to reach senators Vance Hartke of Indiana, Moss of Utah, and McGee of Wyoming. Tom Corcoran's aid was effectively enlisted, and he called Walters from Eastland's office outlining some action to be taken, particularly that of having the railway brotherhoods talk to Moss.

Haynsworth personally gave some information to Eastland. In a letter to the senator on October 7 Haynsworth reported that he had never sat in a case where he had been of counsel or a witness or in which his former law firm represented any party. He had also not sat in cases involving a firm in which his young cousin was a partner. His general relations with the bar were "friendly rather than intimate" so that there could be no question of particularly close association. He had also taken himself out of cases involving former clients with whom his relations were particularly close, excluding from that rule clients such as an insurance company with which his relations were remote and impersonal. He withdrew from any case in which he thought he had a "substantial interest." Judgment had to be used on this score. For example, in the *Grace Lines* case he demonstrated how clumsy reassignment of cases on his small court would have been if he had not sat: judicial efficiency must have some bearing on the decision.[4]

The White House staff also kept active. On October 13 Clark Mollenhoff had a phone conversation with Leon Wolfstone seeking to persuade him to abandon the survey that the American Trial Lawyers Association was contemplating. Senator Cook of Kentucky wrote Wolfstone to "express my complete dismay that your group would jump into this controversy at such a late date." Wolfstone acknowledged that he knew of no dishonesty and no unethical acts on the part of Judge Haynsworth, but he was concerned that there was "so much controversy in the public press" that the Court itself might be injured by the confirmation.[5]

Up to late October business and industry had not become very active. The attorney general then took steps to get the United States Chamber of Commerce busy. By the end of October, two groups of the railway brotherhoods met in Chicago and endorsed Haynsworth.

Haynsworth had no particular knowledge of Senator Thurmond's activity, and Senator Hollings was abroad for much of this time. All of Thurmond's friends were for Haynsworth and there was not much more he could do. The important Senate champion became Senator Cook of Kentucky. At the tail end of the matter, all information on the vote and the lineup was coming to Haynsworth from Walters. During the last couple of weeks, Haynsworth communicated with no senators. "I felt it inappropriate for me to go to those members of the Senate at that time. I made no effort at all. Once the hearings opened, I don't think I talked to any member of the Senate at all except to respond to some request from a member of the Senate. I was doing substantially nothing except waiting."[6]

In addition to good solid ideas, there were the inevitable wild hares.

Mollenhoff believed that a political ring in Indiana was using the bank-ruptcy courts as a payoff device and was somehow using this against Haynsworth. There is no known basis for that concern.

By early November the key question was when the matter would get to the floor of the Senate. Senator Mansfield, the Democratic leader, wanted to bring it up around November 10 and Senator Hruska wanted it about the seventeenth. Eastland reported to the Justice Department that he could not buck his own leader, Mansfield, but he hoped the department would support Hruska.

Professor Wright of Texas led a little group around the country which arranged for individual lawyers in states with fence-sitting senators to urge them to back the nominee. Wright also called to Rehnquist's attention a passage from a 1965 essay of mine on the appointment of Justice Bran-deis: "Overly lusty moral criticism very nearly cost the country one of the most useful justices it ever had. How many lawyers of worth have failed to be appointed to the Bench, at some level, because talk is cheap and charge is easy?"[7]

As the vote drew nearer, the pro-Haynsworth forces began placing more reliance on business interests and less on individual lawyers. For example, in Maryland the Mercantile Safe Deposit Bank was working on both senators, and in Tennessee banks were doing what they could with Senator Gore. Oregon remained a source of concern; the reports were that Packwood was going to be a "bastard." Four or five of his heavy contributors believed that Packwood was trying to curry favor with labor by opposing Haynsworth. As of November 7, Rehnquist's report showed forty-six senators favoring Haynsworth, including twenty Democrats.

No detail was too small to get attention. The attorney general was personally asked to get Senator Hollings off the "Today" show for Novem-ber 13 and get Cook of Kentucky on so as to have a Republican voice speaking for Haynsworth. Mitchell was in Florida at the time, and both Kleindienst and Walters talked to him. Since both senators Miller of Iowa and Smith of Maine had appeared on the program opposed to Hayns-worth, they thought Charles Wright and Senator Cook should be on the show. Producer Bud Shulberg told Walters that it was simply too late to make a substitution; a commitment had been made to Senator Hollings. However, NBC would be happy to put Wright on the week following. Walters kept Judge Haynsworth acquainted with these developments. One week before the debate actually started, Eastland felt there were forty no votes. Senator Hartke of Indiana reported that he could not afford to split from Senator Bayh of his own state but assured Walters that he would not speak against the nominee.

There were plenty of proposals for strenuous action. One adviser strongly counseled that it was time for President Nixon to put the pressure on through his control of both governmental projects and government appointments. While there seems to have been some hold put on the nomination of district judges, there is no indication that any government projects were used as either rewards or punishments. More and more, Scott looked to be key. Senator Fred Harris of Oklahoma put it very bluntly: If the administration could not control Scott and Griffin, it could not expect the Democrats to "bust their butts" to save the nomination.

Pro-Haynsworth expressions also mounted. On October 23 Lewis Powell's well-organized galaxy of former presidents of the American Bar Association endorsed Haynsworth, as did the twenty-three living past presidents of the West Virginia Bar Association. So did the North Carolina bar and the Greenville, South Carolina, bar.

Senator Byrd of West Virginia on October 17 sent a wire to the president: "Exercise some political muscle on Haynsworth. The American people who voted for you wanted a change in the Supreme Court. Many of those who did not vote for you also wanted a change in that court. A more conservative court can do more than anything else to save the Republic from those who would destroy it."[8]

A strong letter to the president urging support of Haynsworth from J. Braxton Craven, Jr., a North Carolina member of the fourth circuit, applauded his gentle and yet effective manner: "Without the slightest tendency to be arrogant or aggressive, he is, nevertheless, extremely persuasive, and in hard, difficult cases I have observed that his judgment and viewpoint are of controlling importance on our court and generally prevail." Walters had urged Craven to obtain a joint endorsement by all fourth circuit judges, which he did.

Meanwhile Herbert Klein, the president's press secretary, got a good and well-circulated statement from retired Superior Court justice Charles E. Whittaker in favor of Haynsworth. On November 15, two days before the Senate debate began, Rehnquist reported to Walters that the reports he was getting were all bad. Jordan of Idaho would be against, Spong of Virginia was the subject of a good deal of concern, and Dodd of Connecticut seemed to be uncertain. On Spong, Haynsworth intervened personally with the suggestion that District Judge John A. MacKenzie of Norfolk might be very helpful. By the time the debate began on November 17, Lewis Powell was back in the United States. He felt he had done all he could do.

A counteracting mail campaign began in favor of Haynsworth, but it was too late to help. The problem was that, working against large staffs, there was no staff Haynsworth could call upon to organize opinion on his side of the matter. While there was word from around the country of a reaction favorable to Haynsworth, there was no central coordinated effort to reach and focus groups. Harry Haynsworth and Knox Haynsworth, another cousin, were doing what they could with professional friends, classmates, and organizations.

By November 4 Senator Griffin was still urging the president to withdraw the nomination; the president remained adamant. In a postdefeat interview, Haynsworth was asked whether he ever asked the president to withdraw his nomination. He replied: "No, sir. I didn't even think about asking him to. Once involved in this, when charged with things which implied impropriety or appearances of impropriety, I thought to withdraw myself would mean credence to those and I would not want to do that." [9]

Senator Mansfield, the Democratic leader of the Senate, had announced that it was time to bring the matter to a head. Mansfield felt that the matter would be controlled by a couple of votes. Now the Haynsworth supporters began to play for time as two previously uncommitted senators, Senator Spong of Virginia and Senator Prouty of Vermont, came down on his side. Spong said that while some of Haynsworth's actions might be classified as mistakes, they raised no doubt as to his "basic integrity"; and Senator Prouty described the opposition as more political and emotional than reasonable.

The next day the National Education Association came out opposed to Haynsworth.[10] As the vote neared, Senator Thomas McIntire of New Hampshire opposed Haynsworth, and Senator Robert Dole of Kansas came out for him.[11] Dole's position was accompanied by a statement that the one thing which had disturbed him was the *Brunswick* case, but this, he had concluded, was simply a mistake. He reported that he had talked with former justice Charles E. Whittaker who told him that it would be "a travesty" if Haynsworth were not confirmed. Senator Herman Talmadge of Georgia declared that the prospects for Haynsworth were very doubtful as a result of "geographical discrimination."

On Tuesday, November 11, Senator Mansfield set Thursday for the start of the debate to the end of finishing the matter on Monday, November 17. *Time* reported Nixon as putting his full weight and prestige in back of the nomination and as being acutely embarrassed because eighteen Republicans were opposing.[12] House Republican leader Gerald Ford began serious talk of attempting to impeach Justice Douglas of the Supreme Court on the ground that he had accepted funds from a foundation which in turn had received money from gambling interests. This was widely perceived as a strike back at those opposing Haynsworth. Meanwhile, Haynsworth friends were writing their senators, and by November 15 the adverse mail on senatorial desks was being replaced by letters of support.[13]

When the debate began on November 17, not many senators were still undeclared. The reports showed that the Oregon senators were splitting and that Senator Saxbe of Ohio was still trying to make up his mind. There was some talk that the price of Senator Gore's vote would be to find him a bull. Aiken was still not publicly committed. Senator Hollings in the debate gave a good but discouraged speech, including a direct signal that Haynsworth would lose. Senator Eastland felt that this gloomy prediction really "loused up" the situation; it was "like peeing in the milk bucket." By November 19, two days into the debate, Haynsworth reported to Walters that Spong would support him, and he was still making suggestions on how to get one or another; in short, Haynsworth never quit.

Indeed, on November 20, the evening before the vote, Attorney General Mitchell called Walters to report that Haynsworth had spoken to a representative of the Georgia-Pacific Company, who in turn had reached the two Oregon senators; Mitchell wanted Haynsworth to leave that kind of thing alone, letting the department look after his interests. The fact was that Haynsworth had cleared the Georgia-Pacific call with Walters before he made it. Up to the last minute, Senator Mark Hatfield of Oregon was still uncertain.

In addition to direct appeals, Walters also had the task of supervising some of the efforts to build up sentiment around the country; after the defeat of the nomination he sent out several dozen thank-you notes to those who had tried.

The formal Senate debate on Haynsworth lasted from November 17 to November 21, 1969. It was set against a spate of press predictions. On November 3 the *Charlotte Observer*, in a screamer headline, proclaimed, "Senator Scott Joins Haynsworth Foes." This decision, it said, would clinch Haynsworth's defeat. The *Washington Evening Star* on November 1 reported, "White House 'Not Sure' Haynsworth Can Win." On the other hand, according to the October 30 *Washington Post*, Senator Eastland, whistling Dixie, was confident that Haynsworth had the votes.

The debate combined the worst elements of the inane, the tedious, and the expected. There had been too long a period of anticipation, too many counts by one side or the other of how this one or that one would vote to leave much room for surprise. The time was spent, as befits an important matter, but the Senate was poorly attended and the result foregone.

Senator Lee Metcalf of Montana put the discussion at the level it was to follow. As he earnestly told his colleagues, he had expected to vote for Haynsworth as a fellow horticulturist. Haynsworth grew camellias, and Metcalf reared some other species in his own greenhouse. From that bucolic background, the senator moved to the matter at hand; he was dissatisfied with the judge's ethics.[14] Moreover he felt that the judge was anti–civil rights and antilabor. Senator Howard Baker of Tennessee, supporting, put into the record the favorable telegram of sixteen former ABA presidents and thought the candidate a man of honor and ability. Senator Dole of Kansas added the statement released a week before from retired justice Whittaker, who regretted the "wholly unfounded character assaults" on Judge Haynsworth.

There was, inevitably, discussion of the standards that should be applied by senators in passing on a Supreme Court nominee. Senator Prouty of Vermont adhered to the view that he would vote against a confirmation only if he had "serious doubts as to the nominee's morality, integrity or honesty," and as to Haynsworth he had no such doubts. Hence Prouty thought the opposition to Haynsworth to be "more on political grounds than on ethical grounds and more on emotion than reason." Senator Edward Gurney of Florida developed his thoughts from Prouty's description; Gurney felt that the objections were "a smoke screen and a subterfuge which has had the effect of obscuring the real, underlying objections to his nomination." Senator Javits of New York had expressly refused to rest his opinion on ethical grounds but instead objected because he opposed the judge on civil rights matters; that, Javits felt, was the honest way to look at the matter.

The whole approach of refusing to consider what was thought to be the judge's philosophy as a ground for a decision troubled Senator Hatfield of Oregon. Why, he wondered, if the president used such standards in making the original choice, should not the Senate do so in passing on the nomination? Gurney's response, basically, was that Nixon had won an election and, in consequence, was entitled to his choices.

Senator Hruska of Nebraska defended Haynsworth's civil rights record. Senator Hollings of South Carolina, chief proponent of the Haynsworth appointment, prefaced his remarks with some bitterness, "for, in fact, the debate was over when it supposedly began last Thursday." The discussion, he said, was simply "an articulation of positions taken." The AFL-CIO was "spreading the poison." He lambasted Herblock for his *Washington Post* cartoons on "Vend-a-Justice." He commented that "perhaps a majority would not confirm the nomination if they voted this very minute." However, he hoped to convince enough to change the result, and he spent two and a half hours trying.[15]

Particularly weighty in opposition was Senator Williams of Delaware, a conservative senator who took a keen interest in ethical matters. Williams was extremely explicit that if he were voting on the basis of point of view, he would strongly back Haynsworth, but he felt that the "appearance of impropriety" required him to vote no.[16]

The *Washington Post* on November 4 contended that the issue was one of candor, claiming that the Haynsworth's statement to the Tydings committee about stock ownerships was not honest. Senator Goldwater of Arizona slapped at the press for what he thought was unfair treatment of the nomination. Senator Dole of Kansas compared the case of Justice Fortas, whom he had harshly criticized, and Judge Haynsworth; as Dole saw it, Fortas had been involved with payments of $20,000 a year for himself and his wife for life, and there was "a vast difference between the charges which caused Fortas's resignation and the allegations of tiny conflicts of interest against Judge Haynsworth." Dole was one of those who felt it necessary to justify his opposition to Fortas and support of Haynsworth; his device was to maximize the difference.

Of course, Haynsworth had critics who opposed what came to be called his "judicial philosophy," but his decisions also got him friends. As Senator John Stennis of Mississippi candidly said, "One reason why I am for him is that I like his judicial philosophy."[17]

At only one point did the debate become as savagely personal between the senators as it was about the candidate; and here the savagery was veiled in the way senators think appropriate. Senator Spessard Holland of Florida read into the record editorials referring to the substantial campaign contributions made to Senator Bayh of Indiana from labor sources.[18] This is an extract from the bluntest passage in the record:

> Mr. BAYH. The Senator has read two editorials referring to campaign contributions to the Senator from Indiana; and both editorials reach the conclusion, or at least the inference that the Senator from Indiana cannot in good conscience oppose the nomination on ethical grounds because of obligations he has to organized labor as a result of contributions.
>
> I just wonder. Does the Senator from Florida associate himself with these inferences and conclusions?
>
> Mr. HOLLAND. Since the Senator puts it that way, the Senator from Florida does think the Senator from Indiana should have disqualified himself and should not have attempted, under his present situation, to have spoken for the interests which are backing him and backing him strongly in this effort.
>
> The Senator from Florida had not proposed to say that unless questioned, but I have never been one of those who run from a question and I must say I have been grievously disappointed in the position taken in this matter by the Senator. . . .
>
> Mr. BAYH. Does the Senator feel, after reading the record, that it is impossible for a man in good conscience to disagree with the qualifications of Judge Haynsworth on ethical standards? Does the Senator believe that if a man proposes ethics as his basis for opposition rather than philosophy, labor, or civil rights, that man is being devious?
>
> Mr. HOLLAND. The Senator from Florida does not look into the mind of the Senator from Indiana or the mind of anyone else. The Senator from Florida simply says that when the record in the Senate shows immense financial support obtained by his friend from Indiana from the sources named, and when the Senator from Indiana has fought the battle of these particular people here against the confirmation of the nomination of Judge Haynsworth, he feels the Senator from Indiana has followed a highly unfortunate course, and the Senator from Florida has said so simply because the Senator asked.[19]

Senator Case of New Jersey explicitly opposed the view that the judge's attitude to the cases before him should not be considered by the Senate. He felt the "ethical matters" not very important. His objection went to Haynsworth's opinions on civil rights matters under the Fourteenth Amendment; point of view was what mattered. Both Case and Bayh believed that the president should have more latitude in choosing cabinet members—part of his "team"—than in choosing lifetime judges. Equally explicit and more detailed on this score was Senator Javits of New York, who believed that the Senate's estimate of how the judge would vote if he were on the Court should control their vote.[20]

Senator Mathias of Maryland in great detail criticized Haynsworth's role in the *Brunswick* case, finding that the thousand shares Haynsworth owned were a "substantial interest"; he declared that for him this was the critical point. He contended that if Haynsworth were confirmed, other judges across the country would be encouraged to sit in cases in which they had small amounts of stock. As Mathias put it in response to a question from Senator Dole, Judge Haynsworth knew what the rule was: "He stated the rule. He simply did not abide by it. And I think that is the ultimate difficulty of this case."[21] In Dole's view, on the other hand, this was a slip; the judge had sat in some three thousand cases and he made a mistake. For Senator Eastland, the matter was regional; the opposition was simply an attack on the South.

Two statements of real importance to the development of the final positions were the favorable words of Senator Spong and those of Senator Cooper of Kentucky on the other side. Cooper was deeply respected in the Senate for his character and ability. In his view, the role of Judge Haynsworth in both the Vend-a-Matic situation and *Brunswick* case was wrong. Both these matters turned on what is "substantial interest" under the puzzling 1948 amendment to the Judicial Code. As he had in the hearings, Senator Bayh declared on the floor that the situation was a result of the negligence of Congress itself and that what was needed was a clarification of the statute.

Senator Hollings painted the "debate" for what it was:

> The record will show that the distinguished Senator from Nebraska is in the chamber, the distinguished Senator from Indiana, the distinguished Senator from West Virginia, and the undistinguished Senator from South Carolina.
>
> With two people on the press gallery, with everybody waiting around for the last two hours to go home, with every senator for the last two weeks having made up his mind, suffice it to say that we could continue to try to make it look like we are making a record.[22]

At the very end of the debate, Senator Percy of Illinois opposed confirmation. He was against Haynsworth on all points, both for his decisions in civil rights and labor cases on the one hand and for his role in the

Darlington case on the other. He was followed immediately by Senator Mansfield, the Democratic leader, who expressly excluded from consideration Haynsworth's views on labor or civil rights; he came out in the negative on the basis of *Vend-a-Matic* and *Brunswick*.

As the matter came down to the final vote, Senator Thurmond of South Carolina, who had abided by the admonition to remain silent, spoke at last and put into the record all of his accumulated distress and the bundle of letters and clippings he had received. The thrust of his argument was caught up in the two-word heading of an editorial he added to the record: "Regional Prejudice." In his view the spirit of the entire proceedings was reflected in a *Chicago Tribune* editorial headline: "The Defamation of Judge Haynsworth." Senator Bible of Nevada, a conservative Democrat, came next, concluding that Judge Haynsworth did not "meet the high standards which it is the Senate's solemn obligation to demand."[23]

Senator Bayh had been the opposition floor leader in the committee and in the Senate. When he rose to say the last word before the vote, he knew that he had his victory in his hand. Throughout the debate he had been urbane; now he could afford to be benign. He briefly sketched the various cases under discussion, never mentioned civil rights or labor, and expressed confidence that each senator would cast a disinterested vote.[24]

On the first round of voting, Senator Dodd from Connecticut was absent. He needed labor support in his next election and at the same time was facing the possibility of Justice Department prosecution for income tax violations. Senator Fulbright passed. The loudest "ahhhh" from the audience was noticed when Senator Scott of Pennsylvania voted no. Allegedly he had made up his mind a month earlier. When the first-round roll call ended, there were forty-four yeas and fifty nays, taking one more to reject. Senator Harold Hughes of Iowa gave it. Senator Fulbright voted aye.

The vote was completed with forty-five ayes and fifty-five nays. Haynsworth had lost most of New England, New York, New Jersey, and Pennsylvania. In the Middle West and the Plains states, a small edge was with him. South of the Mason-Dixon Line he had almost all the votes. In the Rocky Mountain states, he lost more than he carried; and on the Pacific Coast, of the lower forty-eight, he lost five votes out of six. Hawaii divided, and Alaska was with Haynsworth.

Meany was jubilant, with principal congratulations from him to

Andrew J. Biemiller and Thomas E. Harris. The *New York Times* reported senators Griffin and Williams, Republicans, as the most influential opponents of Haynsworth. The vote showed only one Democrat north of the Mason-Dixon Line, Senator Gravel of Alaska, voting yes. The vote was nineteen Democrats and twenty-six Republicans for, and thirty-eight Democrats and seventeen Republicans against.[25]

IX

Postmortems

The nomination of Haynsworth had been made on August 18. On November 21 it was dead. The *Washington Star*, under the heading of "The Anatomy of a Defeat," attributed the result to events of May 14, September 7, and September 16.[1] Fortas resigned on May 14. Dirksen died on September 7. And on September 16 the AFL-CIO lawyers discovered the *Brunswick* case. The reference to Dirksen's death was particularly valid. On September 9 Joe Rauh was quoted as saying that the postponement of the hearings for a week would permit the opponents to expand on the *Darlington* charge.[2]

By November 21 it was all over. Haynsworth was deluged with laments and expressions of hope that he would stay on the bench.[3] A young Princeton student not yet of voting age wrote of his "graceful courage"; total strangers were bitterly disappointed.

While Haynsworth was the focus of the dispute, each side was part of a team. The charge that the administration did not do its best, that Nixon was exercising his "Southern strategy" and really did not care, and that more effort would have made a difference is wrong. The administration started slowly because it quite reasonably supposed that no large effort was necessary. President Nixon pushed personally, and White House aide Clark Mollenhoff devoted himself thoroughly to the confirmation. That Mollenhoff was ill-tempered, inept, and heavy-handed (senators Hollings and Cook thought him more a curse than a help) was a fault of execution but not of purpose. When the administration started to work, the senators were wooed at the White House. On November 14 Senator Jordan of Idaho said that during his seven years of service "few issues have generated more pressure on my office" than this one.

At the heart of the administration's effort was the Department of Justice. There the attorney general participated from time to time, but the major leaders were Johnnie Walters as the political arm and William Rehnquist, usually as the intellectual on the team but occasionally as a vote seeker, too. For example, on October 17 a memorandum from Rehnquist to Senator Norris Cotton of New Hampshire gave him some background material for a possible speech as requested.[4] Walters devoted himself to his cause with an all-consuming intensity. His daily routine shows a man breathing confirmation. He did all the right things. He was effective. There was no careless slippage; if the need was to find four lawyers in a state and then recruit those lawyers to reach their senator, Walters saw it through from beginning to end.

On October 15 Walters sent to the deputy assistant secretary of treasury for tax policy, John S. Nolan, a bundle of pro-Haynsworth materials and asked him to discuss the matter with Senator Mathias of Maryland. He also listed a number of persons in the department to reach particular senators. Haynsworth felt his own shortage of staff keenly; the mass of data he was called upon to accumulate was too much for him and his little group. But at the Washington end, Walters was a one-man army, and there is no evidence that more personnel would have made any difference.[5]

As field forces, Haynsworth's front-rank trooper was Lewis Powell, and two others very useful were professors Charles Alan Wright and William Foster. Powell was indefatigable. As a major leader of the bar in the country, he knew people everywhere. On October 28 Powell wrote John Randall, a former ABA president, asking him to get two or three other former presidents of the Iowa bar to be in touch with Senator Miller. Randall himself had written Miller objecting to the smear campaign against Haynsworth. If Walters wanted to know how to get to a state's bar, Powell not merely had the answer but could reach there himself and did. Past ABA presidents lined up for Haynsworth; almost all would sign Powell's petition.[6] Within the limits of the profession, he was an unequaled power, and it was all at Haynsworth's service.

In a letter of November 4 to one of his friends, Powell said, "The most that can be said against Haynsworth is that he was inattentive and forgetful. It is beyond reason to think that he would have been prejudiced by the trivial amounts" involved. Powell added, "This is the first time, since I've been at the Bar, that a Southern moderate has been nominated for the Court. I think Clement Haynsworth deserves and is entitled to our support."[7] Wright and Foster did the intellectual job, and Wright took at least a small hand on the political side as well.

In the Senate, Haynsworth's case was Eastland's, Hollings's, and Hruska's show. Eastland's forte was strategy and power. Any senator who wanted something from the Judiciary Committee someday had to be really convinced to buck the chairman; Eastland was expert in the uses of power and ruthless, too. Hollings proceeded with absolute dedication. His sense of humor and his sense of proportion made him see things as they were, and toward the end he recognized his obstacles without yielding to them. Hruska was the Republican leader within the Judiciary Committee, but he was not a leader in the Senate, and he simply did not have the power to take his fellow Republicans to his goal.

And how about the judge? In gathering the materials required of him and, more important, presenting them, he was faultless. In four lengthy appearances before the Judiciary Committee, with the lions crouched to leap at the faintest false move, he made amazingly few slips. If he had a limitation, it was his perfect honor, his perfect dignity, and his keen sense of place. In aspiring to a higher office, he would do nothing to demean the post he held already. As a respected circuit judge and a member of the Judicial Conference of the United States, he knew the federal judges of the country. All of them had been appointed by senators. He made no serious effort to use that network, receiving with gratitude the strong support of the judges of his own circuit but not marshaling the others. Haynsworth was a judicial, not a political, animal. It had only slowly dawned on him that he was in the midst of a major political controversy. He genuinely believed that he could be vindicated by the truth, and he did not perceive that in many opposition quarters, his truth was simply not relevant.

On the other side, the winners were Biemiller, Rauh, and Senator Bayh. Biemiller and Rauh marshaled the giant labor and civil rights forces of the country where they would matter, in the home states of the senators; they made the confirmation of a Supreme Court justice a local issue. They planned the strategy, and they worked with Bayh on the ultimate and devastating tool, public relations. By his victory, Bayh, a young second-term senator at the time, established himself nationally as a major tactician. From the standpoint of one wishing to defeat a major nomination, his tactics were flawless. First and foremost, he raised the doubts, and then he kept them alive.

A major part of the tactic was combining senatorial staffs and the staffs at Biemiller's and Rauh's commands to search the Haynsworth record for something to talk about. The correlation of the Haynsworth holdings with the thousands of cases on which he sat was a big staff job. A major supporting leader was James Flug of Senator Kennedy's staff. By the time that staff was done, Bayh, who mastered the work with endless diligence, knew a great deal more about Haynsworth than Haynsworth did.

Bayh's tactics can be analogized to that of the pony express rider who leaps off one faltering horse to another fresh one. The most revealing single comment by Bayh in the course of the hearings was his casual observation to a witness as he switched the dialogue from *Vend-a-Matic* to *Brunswick,* when he said, referring to *Vend-a-Matic,* "We will leave it because we have had a go-around and it is worn out."[8] This was true. *Vend-a-Matic* had been the principal subject of 125 pages of testimony, and it was worn out; as a serious ground of criticism, there is really nothing to it at all.

Brunswick, while involving an insubstantial amount, was at least arguably more open to criticism. When *Brunswick* had been beaten to death, Bayh was ready to switch to the parent-subsidiary cases. A great lawyer's skill is choosing what the case will be about, what issues to play up, what issues to play down. Bayh exercised that skill in the highest degree.

Bayh was a labor and civil rights senator. Those groups could impress senators in the industrial states, but the great mass of the Republican senators who were needed to go over the fifty-vote level were not subject to such persuasions. Bayh needed something more than the policy issue to win, and he made that something his ethical inquiry. Moreover, he handled the matter delicately and effectively. The very labeling of subtle questions of disqualification as "ethical problems" was half the battle. The Haynsworth episodes were basically practical problems of judicial administration that could be resolved one way or another. While there are preferred ways of dealing with them, and they are to a degree ethical as well as practical, by the time Bayh was finished with them, they were exclusively ethical questions, and he was halfway home.

Other elements of Bayh's personal skill and good judgment as to tactics were his care in keeping his written work and major speeches solely on the "ethical questions," leaving the civil rights and the labor matters out altogether. His separate opinion in the report of the Judiciary Committee and his concluding remarks before the vote on the floor demonstrate this. He scrupulously avoided even discussing a topic which could alienate those needed Republicans; after all, there were plenty of others to press the remaining points.

Moreover, he consistently showed respect for Haynsworth and expressly repudiated any notion that the judge was "dishonest." Had he attempted to demonstrate that Haynsworth was not an honorable man, he would have attempted a task he never could complete. Instead, he dexterously let the matter get lost in a haze of "insensitivity," a conveniently misty concept which could be stretched to cover both the all-out attackers and the merely doubtful. Mollenhoff on the pro side approached his adversaries as though he were ramming a brick wall. Bayh dealt with his by going around them. His victory was the triumph of the soft sell.

A third of the Republicans, seventeen of them, voted against their own administration. Haynsworth had no idea at all such a thing would happen—"I didn't have anything in the world to do with this"—but he was aware that during the hearings the White House was losing the two leaders of its own party who should have kept the remainder in line, Scott of Pennsylvania and Griffin of Michigan. On the other hand, some senators who had wobbled ended up on the Haynsworth side. One was Senator Spong of Virginia, another was Senator Fulbright of Arkansas, and a third was Senator Cook of Kentucky, although Cook was only briefly in doubt and early became a strong advocate. Rehnquist talked to a number of senators, according to Harry Haynsworth, and a Rehnquist assistant named Larry Nichols apparently talked to some senators and their staffs.[9]

Harry Haynsworth's impression of the matter was that "the offense was always moving more quickly than the defense and somehow the truth never caught up. The offense would be off to a new story before the defense came through." Harry, in utter exhaustion, would supply one set of answers, and then another would be called for. "We were just always answering." It was "just a constant being on the defensive." For example, one time the judge was asked to produce all minutes of Vend-a-Matic and all of its financial records with some forty-odd companies. He did not have them. He thought they might be at the home office of ARA, the purchaser of Vend-a-Matic, in Philadelphia. Bayh sent someone there and was told they were in Greenville. That led to a claim that Haynsworth was giving the committee the runaround. He finally did find the records and get people to reproduce them. A group from Bayh's staff came down to examine the papers in Greenville and then went back and complained that they had not been given what they wanted. Finally, the boxes were all loaded onto a plane and sent to Washington.[10]

As late as October 24, Haynsworth was still supplying very detailed information by way of brokers' records for Senator Bayh and correcting minor errors as to one purchase.[11] He was very much in touch with the successful effort of Lewis Powell to obtain endorsements from past presidents of the American Bar Association. He closely observed the discreetly ambiguous disclosures of Senator Scott, and by November 3 the judge was reduced to being grateful that the senator was withholding his statement of opposition.[12] To the question of what he would have done differently, Haynsworth replied, "If I had had any idea when I got into it what was in store for me, I would have provided myself with a staff that was equipped to handle this kind of thing."[13]

Senator Byrd of West Virginia described the conflict of interest matter as "a smokescreen" and said that the opposition came from those "who are opposed to the philosophy of Judge Haynsworth." Senator Griffin was described as having bowed to two major Michigan constituencies, the UAW and civil rights groups. Attorney General Mitchell assessed the rejection as "a reflection of the failure of some in the Senate to recognize the President's constitutional prerogatives." He claimed that the defeat was attributable to those who wanted to "get even" for the troubles of Justice Fortas. He insisted that the Justice Department had thoroughly checked Judge Haynsworth before the nomination; the only surprise to emerge during the testimony was Haynsworth's ownership of a little stock in some parent corporations of parties. The campaign for Haynsworth, he said, was conducted by President Nixon personally and by Bryce Harlow, Clark Mollenhoff, and himself.[14]

All Democrats outside the South, save three, voted against the nomination. The *Houston Chronicle* editorial of November 23 put it bluntly: "We fear that politics more than anything else defeated this South Carolinian." At the same time, it recognized that President Nixon had "made some points with Southerners" by the nomination. The *Oakland Tribune* on November 24 said, "The reason for his rejection as a Supreme Court nominee was his philosophy, not his ethics." It decried the defeat as the product of a "vicious campaign of suspicion." The *Dallas Morning News* declared that "the conflict of interest issue has been used as a screen." David Lawrence decried the charges made as a "cover-up."[15]

The December 1 *Newsweek*, reporting the rejection of the nomination, noted also that the president had urged Judge Haynsworth to stay on his present court. A neighbor's three small children came over to Haynsworth's house and sang "For He's a Jolly Good Fellow." *Newsweek* continued: "In a personal sense, the most tragic victim was doubtless Clement Haynsworth. The high ethical standards by which he was being judged would likely never have been applied except in reaction to the Fortas affair. Even his lapses of propriety alone would probably not have cost him confirmation, but they were overlaid by a conservative ideology that turned the powerful forces of organized labor and civil rights organizations against him."

During my 1971 interview with Haynsworth, I put the hard question to him:

> Of course, there was talk, and maybe it was just loose talk, that the administration, discovering that it was running into opposition in its own party and feeling that it had made its southern gesture and that was all that was required of it, figured it could buy peace by not making a militant effort. It used frankly second-level people or kids or others, but the major political power of the sort that an administra·ion really uses when it really wants to go someplace was simply not effectively harnessed and used; the matter was left really to pamphleteering by Clark Mollenhoff and that's about it. . . . Did that happen? Is it true?

Haynsworth's response was: "I don't know, but I don't think so. I think what happened was simply a gap in leadership, and with the defections of Scott and Griffin, I think the White House made very determined efforts to get some people back in line and then there was a counterreaction to that."

Haynsworth knew that a number of senators were called from the White House or in some instances by the president himself and that the president really worked at getting Haynsworth confirmed. Harry Haynsworth was present at frequent meetings with the attorney general, who was directly involved on a day-to-day basis. Any suggestion that the administration was not putting its full power into it, from Harry's personal observation and knowledge, was simply unwarranted.

Haynsworth's own statement after his defeat was constructive. He thanked the president for the honor of the nomination. His "ordeal of the last two months" was over. He asked his friends and supporters to recognize "that the greatness of the Senate as an institution is not diminished by individual disagreements with it." He concluded: "I must now

consider whether my usefulness has been so impaired that I should leave
the Court of Appeals and return to private life. I do not think I should
attempt to decide that question in the emotion of the moment. I will reach
a conclusion as to my future course in approximately two weeks." [16]

Haynsworth was tormented with the thought that if the senatorial
judgment went to his ethics and character, then he was unworthy of being
on the circuit court and should resign from it. He needed to be persuaded
that he was simply a soldier slain in political combat. The letters that
came to him personally from the general run of concerned citizens were
heartening. As one correspondent wrote, "Haynsworth's knowledge of
business transactions was a plus for a judge who had to decide cases" on
those topics. Another wrote urging a man "of your character and ideas"
to "remain in the courts." As one self-identified all-out liberal wrote, "The
opposition to your confirmation is obviously political and I wholeheart-
edly disapprove of this intrusion." Another self-identified liberal extended
sympathy, and yet another blasted "partisan sectional politics." Another
lamented that a person of Haynsworth's character and integrity should
be damaged for political reasons; from another family, "Our outrage is
personal." The descriptions range from "ideological conflict" to "dirty
politics" depending on the restraint and verbal art of the writers.[17]

A weighty letter came from Paul Porter, former partner of Justice
Fortas and one who would be identified generally as a liberal Democrat:

> Basically, we have here a political power play from which our judicial
> system should be immune. In my view, the tactics and procedure which
> caused the Senate to withhold confirmation were both vicious and obscene.
> I think I can comprehend more than most members of the bar the personal
> and emotional consequences to you.
>
> Hence, I devoutly hope that you will not abdicate but preserve a basic
> principle that judges of every level of our federal system cannot and will not
> be intimidated by the tactics which have caused you such personal distress.
> I know you have considered the basic values to our judicial system that are
> inherent in your experience. There are many lawyers throughout this coun-
> try who hope you will not disappoint us but resolutely continue your career
> on the appellate bench.[18]

Haynsworth received a handwritten note from Justice Black, the
senior associate justice of the Supreme Court: "A few minutes ago I
learned that the United States Senate has refused to confirm you for a
seat on our court by a vote of 55 to 45. Elizabeth and I had both looked

forward with pleasure to having you and Mrs. Haynsworth here in Washington. We hope that you will accept this as one of the misfortunes of political warfare and continue to serve your country as the good citizen you have been and are." Haynsworth replied, "My wounds were not mortal, however, and the scars they have left have not prevented my returning to a position in which I can consider my future with objectivity." [19]

Where he could, Haynsworth responded to his well-wishers and commentators. He assured Fred Graham, widely respected Supreme Court reporter for the *New York Times*, of his regard for Graham's fairness. There had been some reporters for whom he did not have that feeling; some had attempted to smear him with a completely false association with Bobby Baker, and some had managed to find some evil in a gift he had made of a house to his university. For these there was some residual resentment, but otherwise he felt that the press had reported fairly whatever it had to report.[20]

The mail kept coming. Senator John Tower of Texas wrote concerning the specious grounds on which confirmation was denied. For Senator Thurmond, this was the greatest disappointment he had had since he was in the Senate.[21] The flood of mail heartened Haynsworth, all the more so because "the great bulk of them are from people who never knew me and, until recently, had never heard of me." [22]

In a very affectionate note to Lewis Powell, Haynsworth had expressed appreciation for all his help and suggested that perhaps now Powell might become the nominee. But Powell had enough of seeing a southern business lawyer chopped up and strongly preferred not to be nominated. As he told Haynsworth, "Like you, I am a Southerner and most of my professional career has been devoted to business and corporate clients, both in the courts and in my office practice." [23] It was not until two years later that Powell accepted nomination as an appointee to the Supreme Court from the fourth circuit and was readily confirmed.

Referring to his defeat a year and a half later, Haynsworth said, "I survived it." "I was concerned about the reactions of the judges of my own court, the district judges, the lawyers in the circuit, and the public in general," he noted. "It didn't take but a few days," he continued, "for it to become unmistakably plain that the judges were extremely anxious for me to stay, and they made this known in a variety of ways, mostly directly to me." The reaction of the bar "was just overwhelming," and so was that of the "public at large all over the United States." [24]

Many senators would come to regret their votes, Justice Black said. He shared with Haynsworth his memory that he had voted as a senator against the confirmation of Chief Justice Charles Evans Hughes, with whom he had later served on the Court and for whom he had developed both deep admiration and abiding affection.[25]

Three future justices of the Supreme Court wrote. William Rehnquist deplored the result and added with feeling, "My one gain from the whole proceeding was a chance to become acquainted with you." Lewis Powell sent a wire to President Nixon, as well as a message to Judge Haynsworth, saying to the president, "This action appears to be a reversion to the regrettable precedent of nearly forty years when the nomination of John J. Parker also was rejected." One letter came from a circuit court judge Haynsworth had never met, Harry Blackmun of the eighth circuit court of appeals, who was eventually to get the chair for which Haynsworth was defeated. He wrote to say that he shared Haynsworth's anguish and disappointment and urged him not to be discouraged, for the federal courts needed him very badly.[26]

X

At Last an End

Carswell and Blackmun

Having tried and failed with one of the best in the South, President Nixon, perhaps to change his luck, decided to reverse himself. As his second choice, on January 19, 1970, the president sent to the Senate the name of Judge G. Harrold Carswell, Florida, soon to be tagged as one of the worst the South had to offer.

Judge Carswell was a judge of the United States Court of Appeals for the Fifth Circuit who had served from June 27, 1969, at Tallahassee, Florida, his residence. Haynsworth's fourth circuit covered the eastern southern states from South Carolina to Maryland. The fifth covered the bulk of the rest of the South; it was a giant circuit, one of the biggest and busiest circuits in the country, extending from Florida on the east through Texas on the west. The key recommendations for Carswell came from William Rogers, who had been deputy attorney general when Carswell was United States attorney and who was himself greatly respected, and from Chief Justice Warren Burger.[1]

Before his appointment to the circuit, Carswell had been a federal district judge in Tallahassee from 1958 to 1969, and for the five years before that, he had been United States attorney for the same area.[2] As a high-school student, he met his bride-to-be, Virginia Simmons, whose brothers ran box factories in several towns, including Tallahassee. Carswell attended Duke University and the Georgia Law School. During World War II he served as a navy officer on a heavy cruiser at the battles of Tarawa, Kwajalein, and Iwo Jima. He married Virginia Simmons in 1944 and left the navy the next year. He then finished law school at Mercer

University in Macon, Georgia, less than an hour's drive from his family home at Irwinton, Georgia.

After graduating from law school, Carswell went home and announced for the state legislature at the age of twenty-eight, where his father had earlier served. Alex Boone, his opponent, is remembered as having had "the radical right vote sewed up." In that area, the older generation of politicians were designated as "Carswell men" or "Talmadge/Boone men" after Eugene and Herman Talmadge and Boone, the person who beat Carswell in his only political race. As one friend remembered it, his election failure showed that he could not "carry on in his father's footsteps . . . showed him that he didn't have any political future here." Shortly after the election he moved to Tallahassee and joined the firm of Ausley, Collins and Truett. A later and greatly respected governor, Leroy Collins, was a member of the firm, which even then seemed a good place to be for a person interested in politics.

After Adlai Stevenson won the Democratic nomination in 1952, Carswell switched from the Democratic party, became a supporter of General Eisenhower, and was rewarded with the United States attorneyship. In 1958, at the age of thirty-eight, he was appointed by President Eisenhower as a federal district judge, the youngest in the country; and in 1969 President Nixon put him on the court of appeals. Carswell was confirmed for the fifth circuit without significant difficulty, although there were substantial enough rumblings from civil rights sources that the Department of Justice might well have been a little less surprised than it was at the troubles that arose ten months later.

The picture of Carswell presented to the country at the time of his nomination to the Supreme Court was of an intensely family-style country gentleman working at judging. The Carswell family lived in a house on a lake some ten miles north of Tallahassee in an area in which, if it had been located on Cape Cod and these had been the Kennedys, might have been called a compound. Various family members lived close by, and some mornings the judge would walk down his dirt driveway to play with a granddaughter in a nearby house.

His hobbies were gardening and hunting; he had converted much of the woods near his home into a local showplace, and he shot ducks and quail from the edge of his property. Carswell had been president of the Cotillion Club, described at the time of his nomination as "an elite, segregated social group that sponsored four dances each year." At the time of his nomination, he was a successful representative of what, in the social world around Tallahassee, was known as the "plantation crowd," a local dominant group living with the comfort provided by cheap domestic service; the Carswells had a cook and a handyman.

Most of the Carswell entertaining was at home and involved bridge playing, a game which the contemporary reports say they played "well, but nicely." When Carswell's nomination was first announced, Justice Black had an immediate favorable response in part because he recalled an evening with the lovely and vivacious Mrs. Carswell as his bridge partner in which he had made seven no-trump. The justice was a bridge player of more vigor than skill, and this was the greatest coup of his bridge-playing career.[3]

About two months before his nomination, Carswell had been the principal speaker before the Georgia State Bar Association and began his speech with an anecdote. "I was out in the Far East a little while ago, and I ran into a dark-skinned fella," he reported. "I asked him if he was from Indo-China and he said, 'Naw, suh, I'se from outdo' Gawgee.'" The local Tallahassee response to the nomination was of pride and contentment. As an old Carswell friend told *Newsweek*'s reporter, "He does get pressured easily sometimes; whatever is popular in the crowd he kind of goes along with, but he won't hurt a soul. He's good people just like you and me."[4]

On January 20, discussing the Carswell nomination with reporters, Attorney General Mitchell, with some suggestion of embarrassment that the FBI investigation of Haynsworth might not have turned up all the information it should have, said that a thorough investigation into Carswell's background had been made.[5] The next day, a first and major problem in Carswell's personal history, not uncovered in the FBI investigation, was unearthed by a reporter who visited Irwinton and took the time to read articles and editorials Carswell wrote when he was publishing the *Bulletin*, a small local paper he had edited there.[6] This enterprising reporter found a reprint of a speech which Carswell had made in August 1948 during his campaign for the Georgia legislature. Carswell had said:

> I am a Southerner by ancestry, birth, training, inclination, belief and practice. I believe that segregation of the races is proper and the only practical and correct way of life in our state. I have always so believed, I shall always so act. I shall be the last to submit to any attempt on the part of anyone to

break down and to weaken this firmly established policy. . . . I yield to no man as a fellow-candidate, or as a fellow citizen, in the firm vigorous belief in the principles of white supremacy, and I shall always be so governed.[7]

On January 22 Carswell, reminded of these comments, said: "God Almighty, did I say that? It's horrible!" In a televised repudiation he described the words and idea as "obnoxious and abhorrent to [his] personal philosophy."[8] The judge elaborated on his point of view at the hearing on his nomination, saying: "I am not a racist. I have no notions, secretive, open, or otherwise, of racial superiority. That is an insulting term in itself and I reject it out of hand. If there be any thought that this be now a matter of convenience rather than conviction, I can only let you be the judges of this on the basis of my record as a public servant of seventeen years, and my private life as well."[9] Much of the remaining attention given the Carswell nomination went to that public record and private life.

The Carswell nomination was announced by President Nixon on January 19, 1970, after Nixon had personally called the judge by telephone. Aside from some brief encounter fifteen years earlier, this was the first time the president had talked to the judge. The *Washington Post*'s response was that Carswell was Haynsworth without the financial problems, chosen for political reasons "because of the symbolic nature of their qualifications." As the inquiry would soon develop, this first impression of a Haynsworth-Carswell professional comparison would not stand even a glance; to put it baldly, Judge Haynsworth was established as one of the ablest judges in the South from a strictly professional standpoint, and Carswell was soon to be revealed as one of the poorest.

The *Post* was beginning to get the idea: "Judge Carswell's performance, insofar as it can be judged at this time, does not lift him even to the top layer" of the better southern judges. "Yet he is the one who has gotten the prize. That tells us something about the President and something about the politics of the day." The *New York Times* was little more restrained. "Judge Carswell, only seven months on the appellate bench, is so totally lacking in professional distinction, so wholly unknown for cogent opinions or learned writings, that the appointment is a shock."[10]

One group which responded adversely to Carswell was the National Organization for Women (NOW) because of his part in *Phillips v. Martin Marietta Corp*.[11] The fifth circuit court of appeals held that Martin Marietta was not discriminating on account of sex by refusing to employ mothers of preschool children even though it would hire fathers of preschool children. Judge Carswell was not on the panel that decided that case, but the loser petitioned for rehearing by the whole court. Ten judges, of whom Carswell was one, refused the rehearing. Three judges, led by Chief Judge John R. Brown, dissented, concluding: "A mother is still a woman. And if she is denied work outright because she is a mother, it is because she is a woman. Congress said that could no longer be done."

The Supreme Court unanimously reversed in a paragraph.[12] It was hard to make Judge Carswell a major villain in the *Martin Marietta* case since he did not sit on the original panel and his sole involvement was as one of ten judges who declined to hear the matter on rehearing. But the case, and the women pressing the issue, bobbed up repeatedly. Its impact was on the time it consumed, because Carswell's defeat was due fundamentally to the use made of time by his opponents.

The American Bar Association committee on appointments reported Carswell "qualified." At first blush the Carswell nomination precisely filled the president's specifications. An early report based on the judge's opinions came from Supreme Court reporter Fred Graham of the *New York Times*, who stated that Carswell was indeed a "strict constructionist." Graham concluded that throughout the Carswell opinions ran "a consistent tendency to view the law as a neutral device for settling disputes, and not as a force for either legal innovation or social change." Carswell, Graham reported, was more conservative than Judge Haynsworth, for Haynsworth had been ahead of the Supreme Court both in some criminal justice matters and in some civil rights cases. Carswell's approach, Graham wrote, was "allowing dilatory school officials to delay desegregation."[13]

As a federal district judge Carswell had lagged behind the majority of his fellow district judges in the South on civil rights issues, and in consequence he had been reversed 60 percent of the time in civil rights cases by the fifth circuit court of appeals. His attitude was caught up in a 1958 observation, "Established law, with its imperfections, must nonetheless be applied as it is and not on the predilections of the Court." It was not surprising that on January 21 the NAACP announced its opposition to his nomination. The Senate, at first glance, thought Carswell's 1948 speech inconsequential. The Republican leader, Senator Scott of Pennsylvania, said that it was a "youthful indiscretion."[14] As prompt hearings began to loom up, the only two potential opposing witnesses were Joseph Rauh, Jr., the civil rights leader against Haynsworth, and Clarence Mitchell, the NAACP representative.[15]

But cracks quickly began to appear in the bright picture of Carswell's future. Shortly after the 1948 speech was discovered, Marian Wright Edelman, a well-known civil rights worker, sent Richard Seymour, her assistant, to Tallahassee to investigate Carswell. He found that while Carswell had been United States attorney, he had invested $100 to help finance the conversion of a public golf club into a private one when public facilities in Tallahassee were forced to integrate. This was a common enough early device for defeating desegregation: the Constitution, as then read, required only that public schools, institutions, or utilities such as buses desegregate; if these institutions became "private," then the blacks could still be kept out. That was the function of the conversion of the golf course in Tallahassee from public to private, and Carswell had not merely contributed money but also had participated in drawing up the incorporation papers while he was United States attorney.[16]

This information was given to Joe Rauh. He, in turn, gave it to Charles A. Horsky, a distinguished Washington, D.C., lawyer who was a member of the ABA committee on the federal judiciary. On behalf of the committee, Horsky and another committee member visited Carswell at his hotel in Washington on the evening of January 26. They showed Carswell the documents and asked him about his role in the incorporation of the golf club. Carswell told them that he had been involved in the incorporation of the club but that he had not managed it or been a long-term member. The next morning, January 27, the day on which the hearings began, the *Washington Post* ran the story of Carswell's involvement with the golf club, although there was no mention of the ABA committee members' visit.

Just as Senator Hruska of Nebraska had been the leading Republican supporter for Judge Haynsworth on the Judiciary Committee, so he was for Carswell. In the course of Carswell's first remarks, Hruska wished to give him an opportunity to clear the record, both as to the 1948 speech and as to the golf club episode that had been reported in the press that morning. The Carswell hearings are 320 pages long and were carried on over five days. By the time Judge Carswell's remarks had reached page thirteen, he had irretrievably hanged himself. Some of the questions and answers:

Senator Hruska: Were you an incorporator of that club as was alleged in one of the accounts I read?

Judge Carswell: No, sir . . . .

Senator Hruska: Did you participate in the management of the club or the writing of its bylaws or any of the background concerning the corporation?

Judge Carswell: None whatsoever.

Senator Hruska: Are you or were you at the time, familiar with the bylaws or the articles of incorporation?

Judge Carswell: No sir.[17]

Yet Carswell had been an incorporator, a matter which he had discussed with Horsky the very night before, and he was extremely familiar with the articles of incorporation, having just looked at them. Perhaps the tension of the situation made not only Carswell's memory but also his wits desert him.

On January 23 staff members of senators Bayh, Kennedy, Tydings, and Hart met to consider whether and how Carswell might be opposed. The leader of this opposition group was Kennedy aide James Flug. In a memorandum he sent Kennedy the next day, he was the first to hit the other note that would eventually ruin Carswell. With amazing insight for the amount of time he had to investigate, he reported to his senator that Carswell was "a mediocre candidate with no indications of particular intelligence, leadership, insight, or respect among his brethren."[18]

This note was developed early on. A January 25, 1970, *New York Times* feature described him as "a judge whose background presents almost no exceptional qualities at all." According to those who had come in contact with him, "Judge Carswell is an extremely intelligent, quick witted and charming man." He had published no legal articles or other writings. For the Department of Justice, "he furnished a list of some twenty-five opinions that read, for the most part, like plumbers' manuals." The appointment, the feature writer asserted, was "of notable mediocrity."[19]

On the first day of the hearings, Senator Eastland put into the record some letters he had received from judges of the fifth circuit endorsing Carswell. Perhaps the most important of these was from Judge Elbert Tuttle, widely renowned for his ability and integrity. Tuttle volunteered to Eastland a willingness to appear before the committee if it wished further information on Carswell's high qualities. That letter was written on Janu-

ary 22.[20] On the morning of Wednesday, January 28, when the hearings
were going into their second day, Tuttle called Carswell to tell him that
in the light of the evidence which had developed, he would not be able
to testify for Carswell. His withdrawal remained unknown for some time,
becoming, like the golf club, another time bomb that would eventually
explode ruinously for Carswell.[21]

Nonetheless, on Wednesday, the second day of hearings, Carswell
was still very much on the upswing. With Carswell on the stand, Senator Hiram Fong of Hawaii, who eventually voted no, began the day by
assuring Carswell that he was worthy of confirmation. At the same time,
President Nixon was strongly supportive of his nominee. Carswell's pecu-
liar memory was revealed again when the golf club subject arose once
more and he observed: "I signed a paper of some sort that designated me
as—I don't recall. The papers speak for themselves, whatever it was designated was there." Again, it is astonishing that someone could not "recall"
a "paper of some sort" which he had handled in what he surely must have
understood to be one of the most important exchanges of his life less than
forty-eight hours earlier. He went on to say, "Senator, I have not looked at
the documents . . . I couldn't begin to tell you what the documents say."[22]
Yet he had just looked at them. When, later, it was revealed that all these
statements were false, it cast enormous doubt on his other statements, repeatedly made, that he did not know the purpose of this conversion of the
public club into a private and safely segregated one.

On January 23, two days before the hearings began, Norman Knopf,
a young lawyer only six years out of law school who worked for the
Department of Justice and lived in Maryland, called the office of Maryland's Senator Tydings to report that in the summer of 1964, as a recent
graduate, he had been in Judge Carswell's court as a civil rights worker
attempting to aid in voter registration activities. He had repeatedly seen
Carswell abuse witnesses and obstruct registration.[23]

Professor Gary Orfield, an assistant professor of politics and public
affairs at Princeton University, appeared in opposition, as he had in opposition to Judge Haynsworth. Professor Orfield had some serious points to
raise. First, in a case involving Pensacola schools, Carswell refused even to
hear black students complaining that their faculty was segregated and that
no blacks were allowed to teach them. He was then a district judge, and
the fifth circuit reversed him and told him to hear the complaint. When
he moved on to finally ordering desegregation of the school after a year

and a half, his plan was so limp that the fifth circuit again reversed him, directing much more vigorous action. He was equally lame in his other desegregation cases. In consequence, schools within Carswell's reach remained, as Orfield put it, "almost totally segregated." In another school district case, he was reversed again by the circuit in 1966. He also had been firm in denying black criminal defendants in state courts the right to trial by juries chosen by nondiscriminatory means.[24]

The next academic witness was Professor Van Alstyne of the Duke School of Law, one of the foremost constitutional experts in the country. Van Alstyne had been a strong favorable witness for Judge Haynsworth, which made his equally strong opposition to Judge Carswell all the more important; he was the first witness to break down the notion that there was any parallelism between the two nominations. Van Alstyne told his story with a rapid series of chopping blows.

First, when black plaintiffs sued to enjoin an alleged conspiracy by the local sheriff to perpetuate segregation in public facilities, Judge Carswell summarily threw their case out of court; the fifth circuit court of appeals held that he was "clearly in error." Second, when four black children were sent to a segregated institution in retaliation for participation in a sit-in, Judge Carswell dismissed their suit. The fifth circuit reversed, saying that the children should have won. Third, when black plaintiffs sought to enjoin police and municipal officers from seeking to enforce certain statutes on a discriminatory basis in order to intimidate blacks, Judge Carswell threw the case out of court without a hearing; again the fifth circuit reversed, saying that the case must be tried. Fourth, in one of the school cases Judge Carswell accepted a "grudging desegregation plan" and again was reversed by the fifth circuit on the ground that the plan was inadequate. And last, in the case involving segregated teachers, Judge Carswell was again reversed by the fifth circuit. Van Alstyne took some wry pleasure in pointing out that Judge Haynsworth, as a member of the fourth circuit court of appeals, had long since decided that very same question opposite from Judge Carswell and in favor of the students. Van Alstyne went on to make one other observation that would loom larger and larger as the days went by: "There is, in candor, nothing in the quality of the nominee's work to warrant any expectation whatever that he could serve with distinction on the Supreme Court of the United States."[25]

There followed a series of civil rights lawyers of good repute reporting brutalizing experiences in Carswell's court and repeated reversals by the fifth circuit. This climaxed with Professor Leroy Clark, of the New York University Law School, who from 1962 to 1968 was staff counsel to the NAACP Legal Defense Fund. Clark made his point with case after case. In the *Steele* case, in an area with 16,000 black students only four of whom were attending white schools, it took Judge Carswell three years to approve the desegregation plan. For a considerable time, Carswell failed to give the parties any hearing. When he finally ruled, he declared that nothing would persuade him to reorganize the desegregation plan and that any further hearing "would just be an idle gesture regardless of the nature of the testimony."[26]

Carswell also refused to enter an order desegregating state parks, which were placarded with signs separating them into black and white. Clark had appeared before Carswell at least ten times and before all of the other district judges in Florida; his conclusion was succinct: "Judge Carswell was the most hostile federal district court judge I have ever appeared before with respect to civil rights matters." He had found Carswell "insulting and hostile. I have been in Judge Carswell's court on at least one occasion in which he turned his chair away from me when I was arguing. . . . It was not unusual for Judge Carswell to shout at a black lawyer who appeared before him while using a civil tone to opposing counsel."[27]

Dean Louis H. Pollak of Yale University Law School had systematically read the judge's opinions and reported them as "at very best a level of modest competence, no more than that." After reviewing all the judge's cases, not just those involving race relations or other civil rights matters, Dean Pollak concluded that "the nominee presents more slender credentials than any nominee for the Supreme Court put forth in this century." Pollak had also opposed Judge Haynsworth, but he stressed that his objections there were based on the disqualification problems and not at all on the question of professional competence; he had felt that so far as ability was concerned he could accept the view that "Judge Haynsworth would be an able addition to the Supreme Court of the United States."[28]

It was at this moment that the fatal error was made by the pro-Carswell forces. At the close of the hearing the committee went into executive session. It voted nine to six not to call Carswell back. The opponents wanted at least a month to build their case. Senator Bayh made a proposal within the committee that a constitutional amendment of his own to abolish the electoral college and institute the direct election of the president, a measure which was being bottled up within the committee, should be put up for a vote on April 24 in return for consideration of Carswell on February 9. Senator Thurmond, opposed to the direct election proposal, thereupon began a filibuster in the committee which dissipated the remainder of the time available for discussion, killing February 9 as the voting date. After a series of parlimentary maneuvers, the committee finally agreed to hold back the Carswell vote for two weeks and take it up on February 16.[29] Senate majority leader Mansfield announced that the direct election bill would come up before the Carswell nomination. This gave senators Hart, Bayh, Kennedy, and Tydings more time to develop opposition.[30] The practical effect was to put the Senate vote over at least into March (in fact, the vote came in April) since there would be a recess of the Congress in late February. If time was what the opponents wanted, they had it.

Shortly after the last committee hearing, at the instance of James Flug of Senator Kennedy's staff, some thirty staffers of liberal Democratic senators met to discuss the Carswell nomination with Joe Rauh. Rauh gave an immensely persuasive attack on Carswell, and Flug presented his own analysis showing that Carswell was a "terrible choice" and could be defeated. How important the meeting may have been is arguable, but at least it promoted the understanding that confirmation was not a sure thing.

The working crew in opposition were Marian Edelman; Verlin Nelson, the lobbyist for the Americans for Democratic Action (ADA); and Brad Brasfield of the United Auto Workers. They had space supplied by the ADA, a small staff supplied by a private lawyer, and postage from the UAW. They began a series of publications, *Facts on the Nomination*. This core group evoked mail from the states where senators were open to appeal. Harris gives as an illustration the effect of mail on Senator Thomas Eagleton of Missouri who had at first been inclined to come out for Carswell but got enough mail to reverse himself and attributed it directly to voices from home. Congressman John Conyers asked for help from members of the House, and Congressman Abner Mikva of Illinois got seventy Chicago lawyers to oppose; Congressman Ryan of New York did the same with the New York City Bar Association.[31]

The February-March gap gave the Carswell opponents the time to make their case. The key was a filibuster against the voting rights act by Senator James B. Allen of Alabama, which pushed discussion of the act toward a Senate recess and, as a practical matter, put the final vote on Carswell over into April. During the last week in February, Judge Samuel I.

Rosenman, a former president of the New York Bar Association and key adviser to President Roosevelt, Bethuel Webster, another former president, Francis T. P. Plimpton, the then president, and Bruce Bromley, a former judge of New York Court of Appeals, had planned to issue a statement as a full-page ad in the *New York Times* in opposition to the nomination. P. J. Mode, Senator Bayh's aide, got in touch with the group and suggested that they might persuade other leading attorneys to sign the letter. As a result, on March 11 Rosenman, Plimpton, Webster, and Bromley, accompanied by the deans of the Harvard, Yale, and Pennsylvania law schools, held a press conference in Washington. They released the text of an open letter signed by 350 judges, law professors, heads of bar associations, and others opposing Carswell's nomination.[32]

Students at Columbia University School of Law gathered Carswell's opinions, mostly as a district judge. On March 5 the Ripon Society, liberal Republicans, undertook to publish the students' results, which showed that of Carswell's eighty-four published decisions, 60 percent had been reversed, twice the average rate of the rest of the circuit. Attorney General Mitchell responded that these were only the published opinions, a small part of the whole, so the students went over fifteen thousand unpublished opinions to show that Carswell was reversed an inordinate number of times as to these also.[33]

By this time very important Republican senators were lining up in support of the administration. Among the leaders were senators Cooper of Kentucky, Aiken of Vermont, and Williams of Delaware, all of whom had opposed Haynsworth and come out for Carswell. The White House also had a telegram from eleven of the eighteen active and senior judges of Carswell's court endorsing him, but the big drama was that seven declined.

On March 19 Bayh called a meeting of prominent Washington lawyers in his own office to induce them to take action similar to that of the Rosenman group. One of those lawyers, John Douglas, undertook to get a letter of opposition from former clerks to Supreme Court justices. Two hundred clerks signed, and other lawyer groups throughout the country, particularly specialists in various federal fields, began to make public denunciation of Carswell as an incompetent.[34] On March 30 former secretary of state Dean Acheson was the lead name of the more than two hundred former Supreme Court clerks who signed a statement which called the nominee "of mediocre ability."

On March 10 a number of senators and their staffs met and established a team of Bayh and Tydings for the Democrats and Brooke and Javits for the Republicans to be the leadership in opposition. It was understood that Bayh would be the prime leader.[35]

On March 3 the *Atlanta Constitution* carried a story revealing Judge Tuttle's withdrawal of his offer to appear for Carswell. This was missed by the press generally. On Monday, March 16, Senate debate began on the nomination. Soon after, Joseph Kraft, a *Washington Post* columnist, was told by James Flug of the Tuttle recantation. Kraft confirmed the report with Tuttle and published the story in his column. The next day Tydings put telegrams from Tuttle into the record. At least as distinguished as Tuttle and perhaps more so was Judge John Minor Wisdom of the fifth circuit. He had not endorsed Carswell; at the suggestion of Flug, a Washington radio station called Wisdom who confirmed that he stood with Tuttle. That announcement went on the air, resulting in major news coverage.

By now it was excruciatingly apparent that Carswell was not professionally very good. Senator Hruska, the lead Carswell supporter, made a statement to a radio interviewer: "Even if he were mediocre, there are a lot of mediocre judges and people and lawyers. They are entitled to a little representation, aren't they, and a little chance? We can't have all Brandeises and Frankfurters and Cardozos and stuff like that there."[36] More than any other single thing this statement killed Carswell's nomination.[37]

On March 27 Senator Fulbright of Arkansas said on the floor of the Senate that he would vote to send the nomination back to committee.[38] Other senators expected to do the same were senators Spong of Virginia, Hollings of South Carolina, and Byrd of West Virginia. Senator Hatfield of Oregon wrote the president asking him to withdraw Carswell's name. A spokesman said Senator Hollings was less than "enthusiastic" about Carswell, believing him to have fewer qualifications than Judge Haynsworth. Fulbright's office said that a number of southerners were deeply disturbed by the "substantial questions" raised about Carswell's abilities. Senator George Murphy, Republican of California, who was facing a reelection campaign in the fall, was said to be ready to vote to recommit. Senator Packwood, Republican of Oregon, issued a statement saying, "There are probably six to eight senators who don't want Judge Carswell and who don't have the guts to vote against him" except by recommittal. Senator Packwood said he was prepared to vote against the nomination. Senate majority leader Scott, Republican of Pennsylvania, said that he still believed that Carswell would be confirmed. He planned to support Carswell, although he "would not have nominated him" and did not agree with some of his decisions. The Philadelphia Bar Association's board of governors, which spoke for some 4,500 members, unanimously called upon the Senate to reject the nomination.

The task of persuading Senator Fong of Hawaii to vote no was assigned to Gary Burns Sellers, a young lawyer with Ralph Nader's "Raiders." Sellers reached an old college friend of their University of Michigan School of Law days named Stuart Ho, majority leader in the Hawaiian House of Representatives. Ho got a resolution through the legislature condemning Carswell. Sellers also reached old newspaper friends in Hawaii and started a vigorous press campaign. Representative Patsy Mink, who had opposed Carswell in the hearings because of his role in the *Martin Marietta* case, built up sentiment against him in Hawaii over the Easter recess. When Fong came back to Washington after the Easter recess, he was committed against Carswell.[39] By late March two additional senators, Moss of Utah and Cannon of Nevada, announced they planned to vote to recommit the nomination.[40]

The real sticking points were civil rights and competence. Senator Bayh finally spoke to the heart of the thing. While the ABA committee had found Carswell qualified, a great number of prominent lawyers, law school deans, former clerks to Supreme Court justices, and faculty members from more than thirty law schools had opposed the nomination, said Bayh. A number of state and local bar associations "have examined the nominee's record and found him lacking." "Never before has such overwhelming opposition to a Supreme Court nominee been evidenced at the grass root level and at the academic level of the legal profession." The president had noted that eleven of Judge Carswell's colleagues of the fifth circuit supported him, but, said Bayh, "one would normally expect all of a judge's colleagues to support his nomination to the highest court. Certainly the Fourth Circuit judges were unanimous in their support of Judge Haynsworth."[41]

Several of the most outstanding of Judge Carswell's colleagues, including judges Wisdom and Tuttle and Chief Judge Brown, did not support him. Senator Tydings observed that "the fact that five of his fellow judges who sat on the same bench with Judge Carswell declined to sign a letter of endorsement is one of the most telling indictments a man could receive. I know of no other instance of a judge nominated to the Supreme Court from the federal bench in this century who did not have the full support of every judge on his bench."

On March 25 the *Washington Post* reported the January 26 meeting of Horsky, Norman P. Ramsey of the ABA, and Carswell about the segregated golf course. Flug called Horsky and asked him under what circumstances he would make a public statement about the episode. Horsky responded that if a member of the Judiciary Committee asked him, he would respond. Senator Kennedy made the request, as did Tydings. Horsky then sent a memorandum, approved by Ramsey, to Kennedy and Tydings, who put it in the record.[42] In the process Tydings declared: "A man who could testify thus under oath does not belong on the Supreme Court. Judge Carswell was willing to deceive the Judiciary Committee of the United States Senate." Carswell supporters, including President Nixon, called the error a minor slip of memory.[43]

Senator Bayh also addressed the matter of falsehoods: "The fact is that Judge Carswell testified under oath before the Senate Judiciary Committee that he was not an incorporator of the club, although his memory had been refreshed the preceding evening when two distinguished members of the ABA Judiciary Committee showed him the papers of incorporation and pointed out his signature as an incorporator." The senator quoted the exchange between Senator Hruska and the judge during the hearing when Carswell denied being an incorporator of the club and pointed out that the night before Carswell had held the incorporation papers in his hands in the presence of Horsky and Ramsey.[44]

Senator Inouye of Hawaii referred to Carswell's 1948 prosegregationist speech as one that could be forgiven—the candidate was appealing to white voters and he was extreme. "At one time or another in our political careers, we have all made unfortunate statements which we would prefer to forget. However, I am distressed by the fact that since delivering this speech twenty-two years ago, Judge Carswell has done little to indicate by deed or decision that his views on civil rights have changed in any way." Instead, his decisions and the golf club matter were all damning.[45]

Senator Eagleton of Missouri announced his opposition to Carswell because "he is a jurist of the most pedestrian and distressingly mediocre talents and with a remarkable proclivity for being reversed by higher courts." Senator Henry Jackson of Washington also announced his opposition to Carswell. "Tempting as it must have been to argue, no senator—

even among Judge Carswell's ardent supporters—has placed on record the view that he is brilliant or exceptional. The expressed hope of some senators that he will rise to the occasion on his appointment to the Supreme Court leaves little doubt about the level he presently occupies." [46]

Senator Hart took up the constitutional question of the relative power of the president and the Senate in connection with nominations. He stressed the duty of the Senate to make an independent judgment and not simply to yield to presidential discretion. On the merits, "a nominee must have achieved during his career, in whatever way, some measure of professional stature and distinction beyond the most pedestrian, run-of-the-mill candidacy now before us." [47]

Senator Walter Mondale of Minnesota joined the opposition with a strong reliance on the Republican Ripon Society's study showing that Carswell was reversed three times as often as the average of the federal judges. Mondale stressed the incredibly high rate of reversals—59 percent—as well as Van Alstyne's testimony, the five hundred lawyers who opposed Carswell, and Carswell's rudeness and discourtesy to civil rights lawyers. Senator Abraham Ribicoff of Connecticut, referring to the Rosenman statement, said, "Never in history has there been such an outpouring of disapproval of a nominee from the most notable and respected members of the bar." [48]

On March 23 Senator Church of Idaho quoted Senator Hruska's proposition that mediocre judges, people, and lawyers are entitled to a little representation and commented, "In all charity, this extraordinary statement should serve as a fitting epitaph in the Carswell nomination." A lengthy speech in opposition by Senator Harris of Oklahoma quoted a *Washington Post* editorial which referred to Judge Haynsworth "in almost every respect a much superior choice." Harris quoted what he described as a conservative newspaper, the Oklahoma *Norman Transcript*, which had originally begun by supporting Carswell: "His record is one of unsurpassed mediocrity." [49]

On March 25 Senator Scott for the Republicans and Senator Mansfield for the Democrats discussed when to vote on Carswell. Late that day there was unanimous consent agreement in the Senate that on April 6 there would be a motion by Senator Bayh to recommit the nomination to the Judiciary Committee, with a total of three hours of discussion to be divided. Following that vote, the Senate would proceed to vote on the confirmation at one o'clock on April 8. [50]

The recommittal lost fifty-two to forty-four. Thus, "the Nixon Administration won the first big test vote."[51] However, three senators, Dodd, Packwood, and Fong, announced that they would vote against the nomination on Wednesday so that if no one else changed his position, the vote would be forty-nine in favor and forty-seven against. The Carswell opponents led by Bayh and Edward W. Brooke said they hoped to gain additional votes from senators who opposed recommittal but had not announced their position, naming as possibilities senators Percy of Illinois, Cook of Kentucky, Smith of Maine, and Quentin N. Burdick of North Dakota.

Even though the recommittal vote on the sixth lost, Senator Scott of Pennsylvania clearly perceived that the anti-Carswell forces had the votes to defeat the nomination. He remarked to this effect to Senator Mansfield. Mansfield went to Bayh and suggested that he move to take an up or down vote on the nomination immediately. Bayh accepted this suggestion and asked for unanimous consent to take the vote at three in the afternoon. Hruska objected, which killed the motion. Hruska assured reporters that the administration would win on Wednesday by three or four votes. According to Harris, Brooke stopped at Hruska's table at the Senate lunchroom and said: "Roman, you can count, and so can I. If you had the votes, you would have agreed to Birch's motion on the spot."[52]

The president's bitterness over Haynsworth built up to outrage over Carswell. On the eve of the Senate vote on Carswell, Scott and Griffin met with White House aide Kenneth BeLieu. Griffin asked BeLieu whether he could think of anything more the leadership could do to win confirmation for Carswell. BeLieu agreed they had done all in their power. It was not enough. On April 8 the headline was "Carswell Beaten Fifty-one to Forty-five."[53]

Senator Burdick of North Dakota was up for reelection and initially had supported Carswell on the committee. He came from a state which had few blacks and no strong labor vote. He voted against Carswell. When interviewed, he said:

> I wanted to vote for Carswell. In the hearings he had the endorsement of the Bar Association and purportedly of Tuttle and Wisdom, and for me that was prima-facie evidence that he was qualified, so I voted for him in committee. But then it turned out that he had this huge reversal rate, that Tuttle had retracted his support, and that Wisdom had apparently refused to back him from the start. If those outstanding jurists who knew his work at first hand

couldn't go for him, it had to mean that he wasn't qualified after all. That's when the torture set in. I really agonized. There wasn't much external pressure. Oh, lawyers from home wrote me, but I didn't hear from the average fellow. I got some burning from pro-Carswell senators, but not much from the other side. All the pressure was from inside myself.[54]

Thirteen of the forty-one Republican senators opposed Carswell. The three Republicans whose vote made the final difference were Cook of Kentucky, Prouty of Vermont, and Smith of Maine.

For Senator Cook a controlling matter was the falsehoods in the testimony. In Cook's mind, if Carswell had been honest about the golf club, "he probably would be on the Supreme Court today."[55] Three southern border state senators voting no were Fulbright of Arkansas, Gore of Tennessee, and Spong of Virginia. Senator Smith of Maine said after the vote that one reason she voted against Carswell was confusion in his testimony about his role in the golf club matter, with specific reference to the Horsky memorandum. "What bothered me was that he said one thing in the evening and another thing the next morning. If he was confused I didn't want that kind of confusion on the Supreme Court."[56]

According to columnist Jack Anderson, "it was President Nixon's most serious loss in Congress, and threatened to stir at least a temporary constitutional crisis between the White House and the Senate."[57] President Nixon's immediate reaction upon learning of the defeat of Carswell was a call in "hotly descriptive terms" to tell Attorney General Mitchell what he thought of the Senate. That evening, Mitchell and the president went down the Potomac on the presidential yacht *Sequoia* and talked the matter over. Senator Dole urged the president to withhold any further nomination until after the fall election so that he could use the situation as an argument for Republican control of Senate. Senator Scott urged that the next nomination be fully considered by all levels of American opinion, including the Senate.[58] The Republican senators had not been told of Carswell's choice until the day he was nominated.

The list of 250 names, reduced to 10, that Attorney General Mitchell had used when choosing Warren Burger as chief justice had become tattered with much use, but the weary attorney general turned back to it again. The name of Harry A. Blackmun, a judge of the United States Court of Appeals for the Eighth Circuit, was one of the ten original finalists, and on April 12, 1970, the president nominated him. The eighth circuit, which covers the states fringing the west bank of the Mississippi River from Minnesota, Blackmun's state, to Arkansas plus Nebraska and both Dakotas, was not southern, and this was a disappointment to Attorney General Mitchell; but President Nixon had publicly given up on southern possibilities.

Mitchell nonetheless looked to two good southern friends for recommendations about Blackmun. They were Hershel Friday, a Little Rock lawyer who, like Mitchell, was a bond lawyer and with whom Mitchell had done business, and Pat Mahafey, also of Arkansas and a circuit judge with Blackmun. Both of them strongly recommended Blackmun, and the opinions of both weighed very heavily with the attorney general. A year later Mitchell was to give intense exploration to the possibility of appointing Friday for the seat that eventually went to William Rehnquist but gave up the effort in the face of American Bar Association resistance. If Friday did not become a justice, however, he did materially contribute to making one.[59]

The voice of Chief Justice Burger also counted very heavily in the Blackmun selection. Mitchell had discussed both Haynsworth and Carswell with Burger, and Burger's endorsement had been important; but in the case of a Minnesota appointment, Burger, also a Minnesotan, was particularly weighty. He knew Blackmun well, liked and respected him, and had common ties of shared experience. Blackmun and Burger had been friends for life. They went to the same Sunday school at the ages of four and five and to the same grade school. Separation came as their education progressed; Blackmun went to Harvard, and Burger stayed in Minnesota. In their years of practice they were in different communities of the Twin Cities. They never practiced against or with each other, and for the seventeen years before Blackmun's appointment they had never lived in the same city or even in the same part of the country. However, they were good friends. Blackmun was best man at Burger's wedding. With astonishingly accurate prevision, Blackmun at his hearings anticipated the future: "There will be times undoubtedly, if this nomination were to be confirmed, when our friendship of the past will be strained mightily because of disagreement. I do not fear this."[60] The Blackmun appointment was completely apolitical in the sense that, by Mitchell's recollection, no senators were involved. Haynsworth's had been to a degree a senatorial appointment inspired by Senator Hollings of South Carolina, and Carswell's appointment had been promoted by Senator Gurney of Florida. But insofar as there was an outside source for the Blackmun appointment, it came from Friday, Mahafey, and Burger; and their advice was solicited.

Blackmun was born in a small Illinois town in 1908. He lived in the Minneapolis–St. Paul area from 1910 to 1950 and graduated Phi Beta Kappa from Harvard College in 1929 and in 1932 from Harvard Law School where he was a member of the group that won the Ames Competition, one of the country's oldest and most famous student moot courts. He became law clerk for Judge John Sanborn of the eighth circuit, with whom he would later sit, and then practiced law with a major Minneapolis firm from 1934 to 1950. In 1950 he became counsel for the Mayo Clinic, moving to Rochester, Minnesota, where he worked for that client until he went to the eighth circuit in 1959.

A Methodist, Blackmun was interested in his church and its many charitable projects. As a lawyer, he served some useful functions for the American Bar Association and, after he became a judge, for some significant committees of the judicial system. He was, in short, a distinguished and respected local figure, far broader in his range of activities than Judge Carswell and roughly parallel in the dimension of his community and professional activities with Judge Haynsworth. Happily married since 1941, he and his wife had three mature daughters, at least one of whom he good-naturedly acknowledged had referred to her father as "an old crock." His family life was very important to him.[61]

The Blackmun appointment was well received. Haynsworth wrote a friendly letter, and there was a small clatter of applause from around the country, but essentially Blackmun was a local figure and most of the enthusiasm was from within his circuit. His senators, his congressmen, and Senator Burdick of North Dakota, an eighth circuit state, appeared for him; Senator Mondale of Minnesota put into the record an editorial from Blackmun's hometown newspaper in Rochester, Minnesota, beginning, "He'd be superb!"[62]

If the Judiciary Committee hearings on Haynsworth and Carswell had about them the elements of a Christian spending the afternoon in the Roman Coliseum with a hungry lion, the Blackmun hearings were a coronation. The Senate had had enough tussle over Supreme Court appointments. The Blackmun hearing was April 29, 1970, and began and finished that day. The most striking feature of the process is that on the matters which had concerned the Senate earlier, Blackmun was almost a mirror image of Haynsworth. They were different people, from different parts of the country on different circuit courts of appeal, but the similarities are more striking than the differences.

Specifically, Judge Haynsworth had been sharply criticized because he had participated in the denial of a rehearing in the *Brunswick* case in which he had bought a minute bit of stock between the time of the case's argument and its later opinion, and he had heard two cases of subsidiary corporations in which he had trifling bits of stock in the parent company. Judge Blackmun had sat in four cases in which he had stock interests in a party, also minute. The differences were two: before Blackmun sat in the first of those cases he had discussed the matter as to the policy of the circuit with his chief judge and had been told that because of the insubstantial nature of the holding, it was appropriate to sit. The other difference was that Blackmun had proved he could learn from the Haynsworth experience. When a fifth case came along after the criticism of Haynsworth at the Senate Judiciary Committee, Blackmun disqualified; on the issue of disqualification, as Blackmun testified: "The times have changed a great deal in the past five years and I would not say for the worse by any means. I know today, in view of events over the past five years, that I am much more careful about disqualifying." [63] The sole event which had in fact occurred on this point in the past five years had been the Haynsworth hearing. The official report of the Department of Justice justified Blackmun's disqualification in the fifth case in the series because "the vote by a majority of the Senate to refuse to advise and consent to the Haynsworth nomination could fairly be deemed an interpretation of the relevant provision regarding disqualification which suggested a stricter standard than had obtained previously." [64]

Haynsworth's conduct, treated as fatal by the committee, was magnified several times over by Blackmun and was not regarded as consequential in his case. The most striking parallel was a case in which Blackmun decided a patent case against Minnesota Mining and Manufacturing Company on December 1, 1960, bought a few shares of the company later that month, and then participated in the denial of the company's petition for rehearing. [65] If there is any difference between the two, it is that Haynsworth acquired his tiny bit of Brunswick stock in ignorance of the posture of the case while there is nothing in the record to suggest that Blackmun was similarly uninformed when he acquired his Minnesota Mining shares. The cases are also identical in that each acquisition occurred when the statute permitted judges to sit where their interests in a party were not "substantial"; the holdings of both Haynsworth in Brunswick and Blackmun in Minnesota Mining, and indeed in the other cases, were insignificant, below the level of trivial.

In the light of the Blackmun disqualification practice, one can only conclude that the fuss over Haynsworth on this score was pure makeweight. The energizing force for the opposition had to be the decisions in the seven reversed labor cases that went to the Supreme Court from Haynsworth's bench and some civil rights and civil liberties cases, particularly the hospital funding case and the *Prince Edward School District* case. As a circuit judge, Blackmun was a little more liberal on these issues, but not much. In two cases in which black faculty members complained of discrimination against them, Judge Blackmun wrote opinions for the court of appeals reversing the trial courts and upholding the claims of the black teachers.[66] On the other hand, Judge Blackmun had Haynsworth's identical experience in another civil rights case; the issue was whether a post–Civil War civil rights law prohibited private as well as public discrimination in housing. Blackmun's opinion reflected the law as the Supreme Court had declared it as of the time of his decision, but in reversing him, the Supreme Court advanced the law.[67] In an unreported opinion, Judge Blackmun upheld part of an Arkansas district court's order on desegregation but reversed the portion that permitted continuation of four completely black elementary schools.[68]

In the criminal law field, the issue was whether two black defendants convicted of raping white women in Arkansas had received the death penalty in circumstances in which a white defendant would not have received it. Judge Blackmun for the court of appeals upheld a conviction because "we are not yet ready to condemn and upset the result reached in every case of a Negro rape defendant in the State of Arkansas on the basis of broad theories of social and statistical injustice." The Supreme Court reversed on a totally different ground relating to the composition of the jury.[69]

Justice Blackmun wrote an opinion for his circuit stating that beating convicts in the Arkansas State Penitentiary was a cruel and unusual punishment under the Constitution, an opinion significant because it reflects Blackmun's intellectual approach to the Constitution.[70] The "cruel and unusual punishment" clause of the Eighth Amendment is a particularly clear testing ground for concepts of constitutional growth, for punishment by beating was common enough when the Eighth Amendment was made part of the Bill of Rights in the eighteenth century; changing standards of morality give a different reading in the twentieth century. Blackmun was called upon to approach the same larger problem of the static versus the growing constitution in an exchange at the hearing with Senator Hart of Michigan:

> Senator HART. But that document frequently, I suppose, occasionally certainly, does not specifically address itself to the concrete question that is brought before the Court. Do you agree that the work of a member of the Supreme Court by its very nature requires some interpretation beyond the words of the Constitution and this interpretation requires an understanding of the contemporary society which gives rise to the concrete problem that is presented?
>
> Judge BLACKMUN. Of course, I think this is saying the same thing perhaps in better language than I was able to produce. This again is why we have courts. Conditions are different today than they were even 10 years ago. I see this in cases that come to us. This is one reason the Constitution has endured, that it is in a way a rigid instrument and in a way a very flexible one. We search for its meaning. Sometimes it is easy, sometimes it is very, very difficult.[71]

In the race relations cases, at least, it was perhaps Blackmun's good fortune, compared to Haynsworth, that he sat in a part of the country in which, aside from Arkansas, race relations problems were far less frequent than in the fourth circuit. In taking all of Blackmun's work together, no one could even plausibly have made out a charge based upon his opinions that he was anti–civil rights in particular or anti–constitutional liberties in general. Nor did anything in Blackmun's experience give any grounds for labor union hostility to him. The great bulk of the labor cases he had decided were routine enforcements of National Labor Relations Board orders. In most instances—90 percent of them or more—it was the union or the employee who prevailed in what were largely pedestrian and legally inevitable matters. There was no instance of Supreme Court reversal of any eighth circuit decision in a labor case in which Blackmun was either the author or on the panel, while in the Haynsworth instance there were a good many. Blackmun had participated in cases favorable to labor interests[72] and cases against the labor interests.[73] None of these were very large matters.

At the hearing there were no adverse witnesses to Blackmun. He was gently questioned for some forty-five pages; he was called upon to reaffirm that he would uphold the death penalty if a state legislature established it, a point of view which was to become more refined by time as he gained knowledge of the complexity of the problems.[74] Senator Cook of Kentucky, who had played a significant role in the preceding two hearings, now had found a nominee for whom he could be enthusiastic. Blackmun had published an article on the right of poor persons to appeal in criminal cases which Cook put into the record; one passage in particular that Cook liked read: "Let us in this entire area, until the Supreme Court instructs us otherwise, be willing to act as responsible judges, to evaluate each case, and to make a considered judgment. If we are reversed occasionally, what does it matter? Our professional satisfaction lies in a job performed responsibly and not in avoiding responsibility." [75]

The committee conclusions endorsing Blackmun were unanimous. The official report consisted of three pages concluding that "Judge Blackmun is thoroughly qualified." [76] It took another fifteen pages for senators Bayh, Griffin, Hart, Kennedy, and Tydings, who had opposed Haynsworth, to account for why they were supporting Blackmun. The two justifications on which the senators principally relied were, first, that Blackmun had discussed the question of disqualification with his chief judge before sitting and, second, that his shares were "but a minute fraction of the total number" of shares in the company. The distinctions they drew between Blackmun's situation and Haynsworth's were more comforting to their authors than persuasive. Senator Hart distinguished the two because he found in Blackmun "a deep sensitivity" to individual rights, while he found Judge Haynsworth "demonstrated hesitancy to eliminate discriminatory practices." One other facet of the varying senatorial opinions was all the same: whether with some enthusiasm or a little shamefacedly, the committee was unanimous for Blackmun.

The committee reported on May 7, 1970, and the Senate took up the nomination for confirmation on May 11. Senator Hruska as a ranking Republican on the Judiciary Committee and as a senator from Nebraska, in the eighth circuit, opened the discussion just as he had opened the debate on Haynsworth and Carswell, with his personal support. But this time there was no resistance; the Senate agreed within minutes that it would vote at 2:30 the next afternoon. Senator Percy was pleased that the president, who had surprised Percy by telling him that he had never met Judge Haynsworth, had had a visit with Judge Blackmun before he made his decision; Percy thought this commendable. Percy, a little sanctimoniously, assured the Senate that in endorsing Blackmun, "the test is excellence, not partisanship, not sectionalism, not philosophy." Senator Scott of Pennsylvania, the Republican minority leader, endorsed the nomination: "This is a good man, and the Supreme Court needs good men." Senator Mansfield, as Senate majority leader, followed Senator Scott with a brief endorsement; he deemed it appropriate to take a detour back to the Fortas matter: "In my judgment, a Justice should not become a casual visitor to the White House; he should remember the line of demarcation that is so carefully drawn between the Supreme Court and the White House and the very precise line of demarcation between the Supreme Court and the legislative branch of government." He saw no problem in this regard for Blackmun.[77]

Senator Hollings could not resist pointing out to his colleagues that so far as disqualification was concerned, the situations were very much the same. As Hollings put it: "The fact is that the Blackmun-Haynsworth parallel is almost word-for-word, case-for-case, former clients, interests, and even cases involving the holding of a stock interest." The senator continued with sizzling directness:

> Mr. President, I insert these cases in the record to emphasize the double standard employed by my colleagues in the Senate as a body, apparently, on whether or not a Judge is from South Carolina or from Minnesota. Apparently, if one is from South Carolina, the standards or qualifications by way of ethics, former client and interest—substantial or not—are higher than would be required of a Minnesota Judge. Obviously, they did not mind, so long as they got rid of Judge Haynsworth."[78]

Senator Holland of Florida agreed in deploring the "double standard" in the two cases.[79] Senator Russell B. Long of Louisiana joined his southern colleagues in pointing to the disparity of treatment between the appointees; as Long put it, Judge Haynsworth "was not treated quite right."[80] Hollings bitterly repeated the observation of President Nixon: "That crowd down there is prejudiced. They will not approve a Southerner." Senator Dole of Kansas more gently concurred with his southern colleagues that the conduct of the Senate was inconsistent.[81]

The hour of voting had come, and Judge Blackmun became Mr. Justice Blackmun by a vote of ninety-four Senators in the affirmative, none in the negative, and six not voting.[82]

What was left was a retrospective on May 15, 1970. Senator Cook of Kentucky took the occasion to look back at the Fortas chief justiceship nomination, at the Fortas resignation, and the three nominations that had culminated in Blackmun's confirmation.[83] He began sorrowfully: "In many respects, it has not been a proud period in the life of the U.S. Senate, or for that matter, in the life of the Presidency. Mistakes have been made by both institutions." He reminisced about the Haynsworth nomination. The attacks not on Haynsworth but on Nixon for his "Southern strategy" and on Senator Thurmond of South Carolina "whom, in fact, [Haynsworth] hardly knew . . . offended my fundamental sense of fairness." He recognized that the labor and civil rights groups had opposed Haynsworth on philosophical grounds, but in his view the issues instead were whether a nominee had "the background, experience qualifications, temperament and integrity" to do the job.

Since, as Cook saw it, there never was any doubt of the ability of Judge Haynsworth, the sole question was whether he had violated any existing ethical standards. Quoting my testimony, Cook reminded the Senate that so far as *Vend-a-Matic* was concerned, Judge Haynsworth had no alternative whatsoever; he had a duty to sit. As for the asserted disqualifications, there was no basis in the existing law to require disqualification—these were "trumped-up charges." The Senate, he said, was "denying Clement Haynsworth a fair trial," and he regarded the episode as "a low point in the history of the U.S. Senate." Carswell, he thought, was simply not good enough for the job. Blackmun "had an initial advantage . . . he was not from the South."

Cook then reviewed Blackmun's participation in cases in which he had some small interest; he found Blackmun's records "a much more clear-cut violation" of the principles that had been applied in the Haynsworth case. Cook became biting when he observed that in a later case Blackmun had disqualified where he had a stock interest. The senator said: "Well, of course, Judge Blackmun stepped aside after seeing what Judge Haynsworth had been subjected to. Haynsworth did not have a subsequent opportunity to step aside in such situations since the Bayh Rule was established over his 'dead body.'" Cook concluded that antisouthern prejudice was still very much alive in the land and particularly in the Senate.

And what else did Senator Cook learn? First, "Let us discard the philosophy of the nominees, philosophy should not be considered by the Senate. Rather we should determine that a nominee is competent. Second, he should have achieved some level of distinction. Third, the Judge should have good temperament; he must not be hostile to a class of litigants or abusive to lawyers. Fourth, he should have violated no existing standard of judicial conduct. Fifth, he should have a clean record in his non-judicial or non-legal life." This, he declared, was his "Haynsworth test."

Senator Baker of Tennessee had a somewhat different view. He believed that in recent years the Supreme Court had "demonstrated a spirit of activism and has at times competed for the role of the legislative branch of our government." Hence, he felt that the "non-philosophy" test would no longer be suitable, for the justices had to be evaluated as "quasi-legislators." Acknowledging that if the Senate were to evaluate Supreme Court nominees in terms of their possible quasi-legislative functions, the Senate must comport itself on a high standard, Baker sorrowfully concluded, "And I respectfully suggest that we have not." [84]

XI

Aftermath and Appraisal

Preoccupation with the Fortas drama did not obscure the vision of those who watch the Supreme Court as an institution. For Fortas individually, what mattered was a visible decline and fall, a momentary disgrace from which he recovered both as a lawyer and as a citizen. After leaving the Court, he headed a small Washington office of a Chicago firm with great success and before long was back at the Supreme Court, an advocate again. A *New York Times Magazine* feature just two years later headed "In Washington, You Just Don't Not Return a Call from Abe Fortas" abundantly demonstrated that his personal lapse from power was momentary.[1]

But for the country and for the future of constitutional law, the consequences were more far-reaching. The Warren Court, of which Fortas had been a pillar, was gone; President Nixon had made two appointments, and the direction of the public law has never returned to the course it was on when the *Life* magazine article appeared on May 4, 1969. Chief Justice Burger replaced Warren. On April 5, 1982, Fortas died. His wife, who continued at the old firm, has done very well without Wolfson Foundation support.

As for Judge Haynsworth, faced with a torrent of supportive mail from all over the country, he wrote President Nixon a few days after the vote. He expressed his appreciation both to the president and the attorney general, as well as the staffs of both, for the strong support he felt he had received. To Mitchell he wrote, "If the venom that lingered in the aftermath of the Fortas affair has now been expended and if senators who opposed me for other reasons are now anxious to show their reasonableness, some good may yet be realized from what seemed an immediate defeat."[2]

Haynsworth reported that he was deluged with messages of encouragement and that he had concluded to continue on the circuit court to render whatever service he could. He was beginning to think that "the travail of the last few months and the action of the Senate, instead of impairing my usefulness on the Court of Appeals, may have conditioned me for even better service. Judge Parker made it that way and I believe that I can do it, too."[3]

Finally, on November 28, he elaborated more formally to the president on his decision to continue on the circuit. He said:

> I have a shining example in Judge Parker, who was my mentor, my friend and, who, for a year, was my colleague. I was with him when he died. After rejection by the Senate on President Hoover's nomination to the Supreme Court, he remained on the Court of Appeals to make tremendous contribution to the development of the law and the improvement of the administration of justice. I will follow his example, with the purpose of making further contributions in the future.[4]

Haynsworth went to Washington where President Nixon received him in early December and announced from the White House that to the president's great pleasure, Haynsworth would stay on the bench. Nixon said: "I must say that after the brutal, vicious, and in my opinion unfair attack on his integrity, I would well understand why the Judge would retire to private life. A weak man would, a fearful man would. The Judge is not a weak man. He is a strong man. The Judge has suffered a defeat, but he is without fear."[5]

Haynsworth on his first day back on the circuit bench signed an order requiring total integration of five southern school districts by the first of the year. The *Boston Herald Traveler* noted that "not once in his twelve years on the federal bench has Judge Haynsworth failed to enforce integration once the Supreme Court set a precedent or Congress passed a law."[6]

Haynsworth's goal was to get on with his work and put the episode behind him; he declined to appear on the "Today Show" of NBC, telling that network that he had nothing to say about the Senate vote other than that a majority voted against him. "Since I intend to remain in judicial office, I think I am firmly bound by the tradition that a judge does not undertake to defend himself or to justify anything that he has done."[7]

The defeat of his nomination led the transformation of Haynsworth from a minor and essentially local figure into something of a nationally and certainly a professional hero. Some public remorse began to set in, as well as some vindication. At a luncheon in the Supreme Court in May 1970, attended by as distinguished a group of lawyers and judges as could be gathered in the United States, Judge Haynsworth walked in. The group rose and cheered him. By 1971 Senator Mansfield of Montana, the Senate majority leader, made a widely circulated statement that he was sorry he had voted against Judge Haynsworth and thought he had made a mistake.[8] Senator Hollings reported numerous others with the same view.

Two years after the event, the judge's reputation had been vastly increased by the episode. "The judges all over the United States and lawyers have been extremely nice to me and quite gracious." His opinion was sought on things where it would not have been earlier, and he thought people who read his written opinions paid much more attention to them than they would have earlier.[9]

On April 9, 1979, Justice Rehnquist forwarded to Haynsworth an article from the *Washington Post* headed, "Reputation Rebuilt Ten Years Afterwards" and noted that Haynsworth had overcome the painful notoriety which had hurt his reputation upon his nomination. Rehnquist suggested that a better heading would have been "Reputation Survived Vicious Attack by Ill-Informed or Hostile Opponents, Continues to Grow."[10] Justice Powell wrote on the same story, saying, "You and John Parker will be bracketed together as examples of senatorial politics that deprived the Supreme Court of two exceptionally able jurists."[11]

Haynsworth continued to sit as presiding judge and then, as he aged, remained as a senior judge on his circuit until his death. He was in great demand on the other circuits of the country and, when he could, sat in many courts of the United States.

There was never a public apology to Haynsworth for the slanders that he had endured, but the United States Congress came very close to it. Occasionally public buildings are named for famous Americans but normally only after they are dead. A highly unusual exception was made in Haynsworth's case. By unanimous vote of both houses of Congress, the federal court building at Greenville, South Carolina, was named the Clement F. Haynsworth, Jr., Federal Building. It was a suitable tribute to a man of ability—and a man of honor.

When asked what consequences he drew from the whole unhappy episode, the judge said:

I don't know, except for the fact that once you are so openly exposed in the public eye—you have been undressed so to speak to the extent that I was, and the end result is a very warm response from most people, it helps to renew one's faith in the American people as a whole and to give me a stronger basis for hope in the future than I think I had before. That was an immediate result of all this. It made the blood in my hair wash out much more quickly than I thought it would at the time that I was being beaten on the head. It did wash out quite quickly. I think I went through an experience which I think was searing at the time, but I think I'm no less a man for that; I hope I am a bigger man for it.[12]

The aftermath for Judge Carswell was not so happy. Carswell, like Haynsworth, decided to stay on the bench; but eleven days later, he changed his mind and announced his resignation from the fifth circuit to run for the United States Senate representing Florida. At the same time, Florida's lieutenant governor, Ray C. Osborne, withdrew from the race in favor of Carswell, having been told that he would get no support if he ran. Some observers hinted that Carswell's entrance into the primary was sparked by Florida's Governor Claude Kirk and Senator Gurney, since the lieutenant governor was not considered a strong statewide contender.[13]

A Florida sixteen-year congressman, William C. Cramer, was Carswell's strongest Republican opponent due to backing by President Nixon. Carswell acknowledged that it takes special circumstances for a Republican to win a statewide office in Florida where registered Democrats outnumber registered Republicans four to one. He based his primary campaign on the premise that his rejection as a Supreme Court justice by Senate liberals was an insult to Florida citizens, who now could fight back by sending him to Washington. In one interview, he spoke of the "dark winds of liberalism that swept away his chances of sitting on the Supreme Court." Further, he blamed an ultraliberal coalition of the northern press and its knee-jerking followers in the Senate for his rejection. The opposition's response to Carswell's scheme was, "I don't think that just because he couldn't make the baseball team, he should be made captain of the football team." Governor Kirk's and Senator Gurney's efforts to win party control were unsuccessful as Carswell lost by a decisive margin to Cramer in the primary.[14]

Carswell then dropped largely from public sight, though he was heard of occasionally as he sought some minor federal appointment in the judicial system so as to be able to serve for the number of years necessary for retirement pay. In 1971 President Nixon appointed him a referee in bankruptcy for the United States district court in Florida.

On June 26, 1976, the Florida state attorney general reported that Carswell was arrested on a battery charge by vice squad officers after he met an officer in a men's room. Apparently, shop owners of a mall in Tallahassee complained of homosexuals frequenting the men's room, so the police staked it out. Carswell made the initial contact with the undercover officer, and they drove together in Carswell's car to a woods where the arrest occurred. Carswell "categorically denied any wrongdoing" and reportedly threatened suicide after his arrest. On June 30 Carswell was accused before a grand jury of making a homosexual approach to vice squad police. He was fifty-six years old at the time, and the grand jury charged him with battery and an attempt to commit an unnatural and lascivious act. Carswell had been hospitalized since the arrest for treatment of nervousness and depression. The grand jury indicted Carswell for battery, but the prosecution dropped the attempted lewd and lascivious act charge. Carswell appeared, pleaded no contest, and was fined $100. He gave no comment to the media, but his attorney said Carswell was not well and probably would be under a physician's care for some time.[15] Carswell's name disappeared from the leading legal directory and he maintained no office. On March 6, 1989, he formally retired as a member of the Florida bar.

Justice Blackmun reaped the fruits of victory. In his early years on the Supreme Court, he was largely an echo of Chief Justice Burger; references were commonly made to the "Minnesota Twins." At the 1970 term, Justice Blackmun agreed with Chief Justice Burger 109 out of 113 possible times.[16] It is not unusual that a few years go by before a new justice takes his own course. This Blackmun certainly did, proceeding completely independently of Chief Justice Burger for many years. Some years ago, I described Blackmun as "one of the real powers of the contemporary court," and this he has been, creative, effective, and his own man.[17] Even with all the floundering, the country finally got a good judge.

After the Haynsworth defeat, there was movement on two fronts in regard to the disqualification issue. I spoke to Senator Bayh, observing that what had happened was simply not fair. If Congress wanted different standards for disqualification, it ought to amend the 1948 disqualification statute explicitly, not, in effect, amend the statute by applying standards in conflict with it in the course of confirmation. Change in the written law seemed fair to Bayh as well, and it was agreed that I would write a draft of a new federal disqualification act which Bayh would sponsor. Meanwhile, Senator Hollings, of the same view, began work on a statute of his own. I was given the task of drafting a measure which would be mutually satisfactory to both senators.

Meanwhile, as an aftermath of the Fortas affair, the American Bar Association concluded to take a fresh look at the whole world of judicial ethics. It appointed a special commission, including, among others, Justice Potter Stewart of the Supreme Court, with Chief Justice Roger Traynor of the Supreme Court of California as its chairman. The Traynor Commission was given the task of writing a new code of judicial ethics. The reporter, or actual draftsman for the Traynor Commission, was Professor Wayne Thode of the University of Utah College of Law.

The Traynor Commission had as its task much more than disqualification, but disqualification became Section 3 of its new code. Thode and I, friends, informally worked out an arrangement for the exchange of ideas between the senators on the one hand and the commission on the other as to disqualification. Senator Bayh and I went to a Traynor Commission hearing held in St. Louis in connection with an ABA meeting to lay out the senatorial view on disqualification. There was no trouble in securing agreement between the senators and the commission that the Congress and the ABA standards ought to be the same—that is, a judge should not be at the risk of violating one of the two, either the ABA standards or the federal statutory standards, while complying with the other because of some difference in language.

The consequence was that an essentially uniform ABA standard to cover the states and a federal statute, 28 U.S.C. § 455, which were substantially the same, were agreed upon.[18] As they relate to the matters involved here, the so-called duty to sit was abolished and judges were given a more liberal privilege of disqualifying when to sit might give an appearance of impropriety. Judges were specifically forbidden to sit in any case in which they had any financial interest, no matter how small; the "substantial interest" aberration which had crept into the law in 1948 was abolished. No provision in the new statute would have required Judge Haynsworth to disqualify in the *Vend-a-Matic* situation; but for the future, greater latitude exists to permit a judge to disqualify if he has an interest in a supplier of a party in case the matter before him should in some fashion actually affect his shareholding interest. In short, the new statute in no way disapproves of Haynsworth's participation in the *Darlington* case. However, neither Haynsworth nor Blackmun would have been permitted to participate in cases in which they had even the most minute interest in a party; questions of more or less interest are eliminated.

The new measure carried the Congress through the combined efforts of senators Bayh and Hollings, Chief Justice Traynor, Thode, and the Administrative Office for the United States Courts.[19] Meanwhile, the ABA code was adopted and is followed in the states; generally speaking, the new disqualification principles are the law of the land.[20]

The big winner politically in the whole series of events was President Nixon. Nixon's victory margin in 1968 was very small; he barely beat Hubert Humphrey. When he made appointments in 1969, he was sending names into a hostile Senate; and at that early stage he needed to be concerned that someone else, perhaps Ronald Reagan, might take the nomination away from him in 1972. Hence, there was sound political sense in the "Southern strategy," or appeal to the southern states. The making of two southern nominations to the Supreme Court helped Nixon in his overwhelming victory of 1972, when he carried the southern states. It is impossible to evaluate precisely how much of that election victory was due to the Supreme Court nominations and how much to other things, but certainly the Supreme Court nominations helped. Former attorney general Mitchell rated Nixon as the real victor in these 1969–70 events.[21]

The entire process, from one end to the other, was hardball politics. The denial of the chief justiceship to Fortas in the summer of 1968 was an enormous Republican triumph for great stakes. The overt grounds of opposition were insignificant—Fortas's relationship with President Johnson was well within traditional norms, and the American University lectureship, while well paid, violated no standards. The handling of the opposition was a political triumph of Senator Griffin of Michigan, sustained by the resistance of southern conservative senators in key spots on the Judiciary Committee who simply did not want Fortas to become chief justice.

The forcing of the Fortas resignation was a victory for Attorney General Mitchell. Aided by the determined hostility of Assistant Attorney General Will R. Wilson and by the creative book knowledge put at his service by his legal adviser, William Rehnquist, Mitchell was able to start with the *Life* article and bring real pressure to bear.

The key factor in the Fortas resignation was the sworn statement of

Wolfson just three days after the *Life* article. Putting together the packet of papers by use of Department of Justice resources and then giving them to Warren created inexorable pressure; two days after Mitchell had delivered Wolfson's statement to Warren, Fortas was off the Court. While it was Mitchell's planning and effective execution which created that vacancy, Fortas played into Mitchell's hands by his inadequate statement when the story first broke and by his lack of wisdom in accepting the Wolfson arrangement in the first place, innocent though it was. Wolfson may have wished to be Santa Claus, but he was not Mr. Clean, and Fortas knew it.

What happened later was political retaliation, a sort of legislative murder in response to an executive assassination. Haynsworth, like Fortas, had his political weaknesses; like Fortas, he was slow to perceive them. In both labor relations and civil rights, Haynsworth was no reactionary. He was not a racist, and he was not antilabor. But he did have a conservative outlook in both areas, and he had a track record of reversals which made him easy to attack.

Haynsworth's fate as a Supreme Court nominee is sad because of the utter unjustifiability of the sticks and stones used to kill his prospects; a frontal attack would not have worked, so recourse had to be taken to character assassination. But these are the fortunes of war. If Haynsworth had not been as conservative as he was, Nixon and Mitchell would not have chosen him in the first place. As is so often the case, the flip side of his strength was his weakness, and this led to the attacks. There was, I believe, no merit in the ethical attacks at all; but by a vote of fifty-five to forty-five, they worked.

The Fortas and the Haynsworth "cases," despite efforts to force a parallel, in fact had only two things in common. One was that each was confronted with political enemies, Fortas from the right and Haynsworth from the left. The other and more important parallel, fundamental and not merely picturesque, is in the vision which each had of himself. That vision was complicated by a disease common to a great many federal judges known as "federalitis." This is a disease which comes from life tenure combined with the exercise of a virtually ultimate power. In some it leads to arrogance (this common vice was found in neither Fortas nor Haynsworth), in others to a sense of being a breed apart and, therefore, somehow special.

Both Fortas and Haynsworth knew themselves to be absolutely honest. The most revealing single comment Judge Haynsworth ever made in my own presence, anent some suspected impropriety of someone else, was a murmured, "We wouldn't do that in the fourth circuit." There is a self-sufficiency to this gentlemanly integrity and an unawareness that others may see things differently. Fortas, when he made the Wolfson arrangement, and in the infinitely more trivial instance Haynsworth, when he reached the final stages of *Brunswick*, set themselves up as delayed victims of that unawareness.

Carswell must be viewed historically as a bad legal joke. Like Fortas, he helped to dig his own grave with his mouth. Want of candor to a senatorial committee is rarely rewarded, and Carswell was almost disgustingly wanting in candor. But he was so demonstrably incompetent that he might well have lost no matter how much truth he told; and I believe that he, unlike Haynsworth, really was a racist. Political triumph in Carswell's case goes partly to the senators, particularly to Senator Bayh, but also very markedly to Joseph Rauh and Marian Edelman, the civil rights leaders who organized the country.

The Blackmun confirmation made the Haynsworth pretense transparent. If one starts from the wholly fallacious premise that Haynsworth was either unethical or insensitive, then Blackmun not merely duplicated but multiplied the Haynsworth sins. The truth, of course, is that neither of them in this respect did anything wrong under the law as it stood. Beyond the similarities, there were differences; while Blackmun was no flaming liberal, he showed a better face to labor than did Haynsworth, and with less opportunity than Haynsworth to be involved in civil rights matters, he at least looked less forbidding to civil rights interests.

What of the Court and the country? The run of events has been approximately the same with Blackmun and the Court as if Haynsworth had been confirmed, so far as these mysterious things can be known. The two are not interchangeable; but only a year later, President Nixon got his southern appointment when he designated Lewis Powell of Richmond. Powell had been Haynsworth's staunchest supporter outside the government. Powell was truly sad that Haynsworth, a southeasterner from a state so near to his own, had to be slaughtered so that he could be appointed. The going can be tough for the first one.

In 1987 Powell retired with the observation, "There was *de jure* segregation in the Southern states, not only of the schools but of public accommodations, facilities, theaters. I just can't imagine how I grew up and accepted that as a normal way of life in this country."[22] Haynsworth would doubtless have had similar experience.

While Blackmun for a time served as a Burger echo, he has clearly been his own creative force for many years. If the country had kept Fortas for the balance of Fortas's life, our constitutional law would be definably different; but the most remarkable feature of the run of Nixon appointments is how little a break they made with the traditions of the past.

What passes on for the future is the question left unresolved in the Cook-Baker retrospective after the Blackmun appointment. Senator Cook surely expressed what had been a majority spoken view for many years, that the criteria for a senator voting on a nomination should be the competence, integrity, distinction, and ability of the nominee, but not his point of view. Senator Baker, with his counter that the Court had become so large a part of the policy-making machinery of the country that a nominee's point of view must be considered as well, stated the criteria that in fact controlled the forcing out of Fortas and the defeats of Haynsworth and Carswell. A memorandum from then Assistant Attorney General Rehnquist to Senator Eastland on September 9, 1969, recorded that in the Fortas chief justice debate almost every senator was arguing philosophy. Seventeen years later, Rehnquist was to be subjected to the same experience.

As an aftermath of these events, it may be that the approach which stresses only the quality of a Court nominee has become an exercise in lip service, an invocation of a world in which we once lived but do not now. It may also be that Baker was right, that just as war is too important to be left to generals, so Supreme Court judging is too important to be left to the merely professionally able.

That debate remained unresolved until the nomination of Judge Robert Bork to the Supreme Court in 1987. In Bork's case, any pretense of excluding from consideration the philosophy of a nominee vanished; a large number of senators thought Bork's views too extreme to be acceptable. A tide rising with the 1969–70 nominations engulfed the 1987 nomination. By now, the heavy weight of the Senate is set to resist what it regards, rightly or wrongly, as extremism in a Supreme Court nominee.

Notes

I. The Fortas Vacancy

1. *Durham v. United States,* 214 F.2d 862 (D.C. Cir. 1954) (insanity); *Gideon v. Wainright,* 372 U.S. 335 (1963) (right to counsel).

2. One of the best extended articles on Fortas is Fred Graham's "The Many-Sided Justice Fortas," *New York Times Magazine,* June 4, 1967.

3. Leonard Baker, *Brandeis and Frankfurter* (New York: Harper & Row, 1984), 147–48; A. T. Mason, *William Howard Taft* (New York: Simon & Schuster, 1964), 138; A. T. Mason, *Harlan Fiske Stone* (New York: Viking Press, 1956), 270.

4. *Senate Executive Report No. 8,* 90th Cong., 2d sess., 1968, 5–6.

5. The minutes of the Wolfson Foundation, Dec. 28, 1965, show the appointment of Fortas as an adviser to the Foundation, a position Wolfson reported Fortas had agreed orally to accept. Fortas confirmed in writing on Jan. 10, and the arrangement was approved in a joint writing of Feb. 1, 1966, including the provision, "We undertake to pay you $20,000 per annum for your life" and "payments would be continued to Mrs. Fortas for her life if she should survive you" (Earl Warren MSS, Library of Congress).

6. Robert Shogan, *A Question of Judgment* (Indianapolis: Bobbs Merrill Co., 1972), 185–86.

7. Ibid., 209.

8. Warren MSS, Lib. Cong.

9. Shogan, 212.

10. Ibid., 231–32.

11. Wolfson was present and introduced Fortas who "spoke at length" concerning the juvenile justice project he was undertaking for the foundation (Foundation minutes, June 15, 1966, meeting, Warren MSS, Lib. Cong.).

12. Shogan (236) puts it accurately: "Of all the thousands of words printed and uttered about the case that followed, none were so damaging to Fortas as the

300 that issued from his own hand on Sunday afternoon." The text is reprinted in Shogan, 277.

13. *New York Times*, May 6, 1969, 1, May 8, 1969, 34, May 9, 1969, 12, May 12, 1969, 1, May 13, 1969, 1, May 15, 1969, 46.

14. Former Attorney General John Mitchell, interview with author, Washington, D.C., May 20, 1987.

15. On May 14, 1969, the day the justice resigned, Chief Justice Warren returned to Mitchell "all of the documents which you personally delivered to and discussed with me on May 7" and the May 12 documents, including a list of each set; but he put a copy of his letter of return into his files, along with copies of the documents (Warren MSS, Lib. Cong.).

16. Laura Kalman, *Abe Fortas* (New Haven: Yale Univ. Press, 1990), 372; May 5, 1969, *Congressional Record* (hereafter *Cong. Rec.*), 91st Cong., 1st sess., 1969, 11209 (Rep. Gross), 11222 (Rep. Scherle), 11259 (Sen. Miller), 11260 (Sen. Williams).

17. Shogan, 242, 244.

18. Discussion, author with Clifford after Douglas's death.

19. Mason, *William Howard Taft*, 274.

20. Letter, Brennan to author, Jan. 20, 1987.

21. Fortas to Mrs. Warren, June 11, 1969, Warren MSS, Lib. Cong.

22. Fortas to Chief Justice Warren, May 14, 1969, ibid.

23. Discussion with Freund, May, 1969.

24. *New York Post*, May 17, 1969, Magazine sec. 51.

25. Editorial, *New York Times*, May 16, 1969, 45C.

26. Editorial, *Washington Post*, May 6, 1969, A18.

27. Ibid., May 16, 1969, A1.

II. Haynsworth and the Circuit Judgeship

1. The basic biographical facts about Haynsworth are taken from Federal Bureau of Investigation reports obtained from the Department of Justice under the Freedom of Information Act (hereafter FOIA) on the Haynsworth nomination and from the *Washington Post*'s Aug. 19, 1969, account on his nomination.

2. For full genealogical data on the Haynsworth and Furman families, see Hugh C. Haynsworth, *Ancestry and Decendants of Sarah Morse Haynsworth* (Sumter, S.C.: Osteen Pub. Co., 1939) and a second volume by the same author and publisher, *Haynsworth-Furman and Allied Families* (1942).

3. Haynsworth to Sen. Ervin, Nov. 4, 1970, Haynsworth collection, Furman University, Greenville, S.C. (hereafter Furman MSS).

4. *Annual Report of the Director of the Administrative Office of the U.S. Courts* (Washington, D.C.: GPO, 1957), 72–73.

5. Ibid., 1968, 184.

6. A rare collection of leading Haynsworth opinions is the volume published

privately by his law clerks on his thirtieth anniversary on the court of appeals, 1987, with an analytical introduction by Prof. Charles Alan Wright, *Clement Furman Haynsworth, Jr.* (Washington, D.C.: D.C. Press, 1987).

7. *Long Manufacturing Co. v. Holliday,* 246 F.2d 95 (4th Cir. 1957).

8. *Markham v. City of Newport News,* 292 F.2d 711 (4th Cir. 1961).

9. *Baines v. City of Danville, Virginia,* 337 F.2d 579 (4th Cir. 1964) (en banc).

10. *Switzerland Co. v. Udall,* 337 F.2d 56 (4th Cir. 1964).

11. The Haynsworth opinion is *Rowe v. Peyton,* 383 F.2d 709 (4th Cir. 1967), and the confirming opinion of Chief Justice Warren for a unanimous Supreme Court is reported at 391 U.S. 54, 57 (1968).

12. *United States v. Chandler,* 393 F.2d 920 (4th Cir. 1968); *Wratchford v. S. J. Groves & Sons Company,* 405 F.2d 1061 (4th Cir. 1969). My description of Haynsworth's opinions draws on Charles Alan Wright's introduction to *Clement Furman Haynsworth, Jr.*

13. Senate Committee on the Judiciary, *Hearings on the Nomination of Clement Haynsworth to the Supreme Court of the United States,* 91st Cong., 1st sess., Sept. 16–26, 1969, 199–207 (hereafter *H.*).

14. For a more sympathetic analysis of these cases, see *H.,* 384–90; there were dozens of cases in which Judge Haynsworth had voted for unions and against employers (*H.,* 389–90).

15. Judge Haynsworth's opinion is *NLRB v. S.S. Logan Packing Co.,* 386 F.2d 562 (4th Cir. 1967), and the Supreme Court opinion reversing this legal position is *NLRB v. Gissel Packing Co.,* 395 U.S. 575 (1969).

16. 323 F.2d 959 (1963).

17. 322 F.2d 332 (1963).

18. *H.,* 433.

19. For a collection of at least a dozen, see *H.,* 448–49.

20. *Washington Post,* Aug. 24, 1969, A8. A review of the minutes of Vend-a-Matic show that it was organized in 1956 with Haynsworth as a director and vice president. The minutes carried him as vice president through 1962. They also show that he resigned effective Oct. 15, 1963.

21. The court of appeals opinion, not written but joined in by Judge Haynsworth, is reported at 325 F.2d 682 (4th Cir. 1963); the Supreme Court decision is reported at 380 U.S. 263 (1965).

22. All papers, from the beginning to the Robert Kennedy letter, are collected with Memorandum of senators Eastland and Hruska relating to Department of Justice file, *H.,* 2–19.

III. The Supreme Court Appointment

1. Mitchell interview, Washington, D.C., May 20, 1987.

2. Hollings to Nixon, May 28, 1969, from papers supplied on request by the Department of Justice under the FOIA.

3. Furman MSS. There were, of course, volunteer letters unprovoked by the judge (ibid.). For example, on July 9, 1969, Prof. Charles Alan Wright, University of Texas Law School, wrote Attorney General Mitchell urging the Haynsworth appointment as "a splendid addition to the Court" (Wright collection made available to author).

4. FBI reports, FOIA.

5. Mitchell confirmed this. At the Department of Justice when the Burger appointment was announced, Nina Totenberg, a hostile reporter, asked Mitchell, "Where did you find Burger?" Mitchell replied, "Central casting," a reference to Burger's splendidly judicial appearance, which ended that discussion (Mitchell interview, Washington, D.C., May 20, 1987).

6. Judge Haynsworth and Harry Haynsworth, interview with author, Hot Springs, Va., June 26, 1971 (hereafter 1971 interview), to be deposited in the Library of Congress upon publication of this book, as he wished.

7. Ibid.

8. Ibid.

9. Walters to Mitchell, FOIA.

10. Furman MSS.

11. 1971 interview.

12. Ibid.

13. *Washington Post*, Aug. 19, 1969.

14. At the time of the Haynsworth appointment, Russell was a federal district judge. There was widespread newspaper specualtion that he would obtain the Haynsworth seat on the court of appeals. Russell had opposed Hollings for the Senate in a very bitter campaign, but speculation that Hollings might oppose Russell was set at rest by an early leak from the Hollings office that he would not do so.

15. Department of Justice, FOIA. The *Darlington* case was referred to variously as *Darlington*, the actual party, or *Vend-a-Matic*, the name of the vending company once partly owned by Haynsworth. Since Darlington was a subsidiary of *Deering-Milliken*, the case was also called *Deering-Milliken*.

16. Furman MSS.

17. Wright to Haynsworth, Aug. 18, 1969, ibid. and Wright collection.

18. Furman MSS.

19. Ibid., Aug. 19, 20, 21, 1969.

20. *U.S. News and World Report*, Aug. 25, 1969, 14.

21. Furman MSS.

22. *Time*, Aug. 29, 1969, 11.

23. Furman MSS.

24. *Newsweek*, July 28, 1969, 40.

25. *Time*, Aug. 29, 1969, 11, 12. As *Time* accurately reported, the big news of the appointment was that "for the first time since 1956 the activist, liberal coalition led by Justices Black, Douglas, Brennan and Marshall is a minority."

26. *Arizona Republic*, Sept. 3, 1969.

27. From a nine-box collection, Senate Judiciary Committee (the boxes are

not clearly numbered; this is apparently either box 8 or 9 and has a small x on the upper left corner). In verbal parallel, Jesse Scott, field director of the NAACP for Southern California, wired the Senate Judiciary Committee that Haynsworth was "unfit to be an Associate Justice of the United States Supreme Court" (telegram, Scott to Senate Judiciary, Oct. 6, 1969, Sen. Jud. files).

28. *Time*, Sept. 26, 1969, 21.

29. Department of Justice, FOIA.

30. *Fortune*, March 1970.

31. *Newsweek*, Oct. 20, 1969, 36.

32. This and the following paragraphs are drawn from the 1971 interview.

33. *AFL-CIO News*, Aug. 30, 1969.

34. Walters MSS, in my possession but to be deposited with the Library of Congress upon publication of this book (hereafter Walters MSS).

35. 1971 interview.

IV. The Judiciary Committee: *Darlington* and Disqualification

1. Wright to author, undated.

2. *Washington Evening Star*, Sept. 9, 1969.

3. *Washington Post*, Sept. 10, 1969, A-11.

4. For a comprehensive labor attack on the Vend-a-Matic matter, see *AFL-CIO News*, Washington, D.C., Aug. 30, 1969, 12. As of Sept. 9, 1969, the Department of Justice wrote Lawrence E. Walsh, chairman of the ABA committee on nominations, on the schedule for the hearings. This listed essentially the people who did testify favorably and those who testified in opposition, including the AFL-CIO and the NAACP. A supplemental list of Sept. 16 broadened the list, but by that time the plan was completely stabilized.

5. *H.,* 25.

6. *Fortune*, March 1970, 155.

7. *Columbia, S.C., Record*, Sept. 15, 1969.

8. *Columbia State*, Sept. 14, 1969.

9. Walters MSS.

10. *H.,* 37. In these introductory remarks the senator observed: "There is no more eminent authority on judicial ethics than Prof. John P. Frank, formerly of Yale University, and now in Phoenix, Ariz. He is here and will testify, and I am sure he will explain to your satisfaction the Judge's duty to sit on the case" (*H.,* 38).

11. *H.,* 39–41, for Haynsworth's preliminary description of *Vend-a-Matic*.

12. *H.,* 42.

13. *H.,* 44 (McClellan), 49 (Ervin).

14. These comments are found at *H.,* 58, 59.

15. *H.,* 61–63.

16. 334 F.2d 360, 362–63 (5th Cir. 1964).

17. *H.,* 64.

18. *H.*, 65.

19. *H.*, 99.

20. *H.*, 103.

21. *H.*, 105.

22. *H.*, 484.

23. *H.*, 112.

24. For example, it is reported that the distinguished court of appeals judge Learned Hand, in jocund mood, would tell counsel that he had twenty-five shares of stock in Westinghouse and ask whether they would like him to step off the bench in a Westinghouse case. This practice, described by me as a "velvet black-jack," a phrase picked up by Jack MacKenzie of the *New York Times* who wrote a book on that subject, gave the attorney, who would need to be back before the judge frequently on other matters, very little real option, and the waiver practice is now largely eliminated from the law.

25. *H.*, 115.

26. *H.*, 123.

27. 392 F.2d 327 (4th Cir. 1968).

28. *H.*, 132.

29. *Washington Post*, Sept. 22, 1969, A20.

30. *Time*, Sept. 26, 1969, 21.

31. 1971 interview.

32. Walters MSS.

33. Senate Judiciary Committee Records.

34. *H.*, 153.

35. Walters MSS; Department of Justice, FOIA.

36. McCall, *H.*, 263, 270.

37. I have always supposed that this was not a fortuity and that the fifth circuit was timing its stand with an eye to the nomination controversy; but this is supposition and I have no facts.

38. *Kinnear-Weed Corp. v. Humble Oil and Refining Co.*, 403 F.2d 437 (5th Cir. 1968); *Austral Oil Co., Inc. v. Federal Power Commission*, 560 F.2d 1262 (5th Cir. 1969).

39. *H.*, 66.

40. *H.*, 68.

41. *H.*, 61, 94.

42. *H.*, 70, 71.

43. 1971 interview.

44. Ibid.

V. Interlude: The Outlook of Judge Haynsworth

1. Furman MSS, Sept. 13, 1969.

2. *H.*, 75.

3. *H.*, 75.
4. *H.*, 75.
5. *H.*, 76.
6. *H.*, 76.
7. *H.*, 79.

VI. The Attack

1. *H.*, 80.
2. *H.*, 92.
3. *H.*, 99.
4. 1971 interview. Haynsworth, in fact, had a largely bad press. An illustration is an editorial, *St. Louis Post Dispatch*, Oct. 6, 1969: "Judge Haynsworth's business dealings show him to be insensitive to the extraordinarily high standard that ought to apply to the Supreme Court while his record of reversal on civil rights issues shows him to be on the wrong side too often. He is a mediocre man, lacking the distinction to qualify for the high tribunal."
5. Furman MSS.
6. *H.*, 270.
7. *H.*, 271.
8. *H.*, 271–72.
9. *H.*, 272.
10. *H.*, 286.
11. *H.*, 292.
12. *H.*, 301, 303.
13. *H.*, 163.
14. *H.*, 170.
15. *H.*, 173.
16. *H.*, 176, 187.
17. *H.*, 215, 231. The relevance of Fine's Jewishness is that for thirty-three years there had been at least one Jewish justice on the Court, and with the departure of Fortas, there was none; some minor point was made of this in the discussion.
18. *Simkins v. Moses H. Cone Memorial Hospital*, 323 F.2d 959 (4th Cir. 1963).
19. *Eaton v. Grubbs*, 329 F.2d 710 (4th Cir. 1964).
20. *Griffin v. Bd. of Supervisors*, 322 F.2d 332 (4th Cir., 1963).
21. *H.*, 446.
22. *H.*, 457.
23. *Bowman v. County School Board*, 382 F.2d 326 (4th Cir. 1967), *reversed*, 391 U.S. 430 (1968).
24. *H.*, 465.
25. *H.*, 590, 593.

26. *H.*, 602.

27. *H.*, 612.

28. Sept. 27, 1969.

VII. Senatorial Slugging Match

1. *Columbia State*, Oct. 10, 1969.

2. *U.S. News and World Report*, Oct. 6, 1969, 76.

3. Department of Justice, FOIA, and Wright collection.

4. *Columbia Record*, Oct. 4, 1969.

5. *Columbia State*, Oct. 6, 1969.

6. *Columbia Record*, Oct. 3, 1969.

7. KTAR Broadcast, "Paul Harvey News," Oct. 4, 1969.

8. Ibid.

9. Memorandum to the Assistant to the President from Rehnquist, Sept. 30, 1969, Department of Justice, FOIA. Haynsworth had met Baker only three times in his life, the most recent being more than ten years before his nomination (1971 interview).

10. *Cong. Rec.*, 91st Cong., 1st sess., 1969, S.12069.

11. Sen. Hollings to Sen. Jordan, Oct. 8, 1969; the same letter went to the other senators. Hollings added, "I have proposed a bill to clarify the requirement of judges providing that they have no investment whatever in a party before them. I would appreciate your co-sponsorship" (Furman MSS). After the fight was over, Sen. Bayh, Sen. Hollings, and I joined in obtaining just such legislation, supported by many senators; see Chapter XI below.

12. *Farrow v. Grace Lines, Inc.*, 381 F.2d 380 (4th Cir. 1967). *Grace* was a case in which Haynsworth held a little stock in a holding company of a party.

13. *Time*, Oct. 10, 1969, 15.

14. ATLA reported that 73 percent of its members polled opposed the nomination and that, therefore, it did too (*Columbia Record*, Oct. 27, 1969, sec. BP1).

15. Ibid., Oct. 9, 1969.

16. *Time*, Oct. 10, 1969, 15.

17. Ibid., 17.

18. Walters MSS.

19. For a report on the Republican Chairmen's meeting, see *Columbia State*, Oct. 23, 1969.

20. *Newsweek*, Oct. 20, 1969, 35–36.

21. Ibid.

22. Ibid., Oct. 27, 1969, 36.

23. Richard P. Nelson, Assistant to Sen. Hruska, to Harry J. Haynsworth, Nov. 12, 1969, Furman MSS.

24. The ten were five Democrats (Eastland, McDillon, Ervin, Dodd, and Byrd of W.Va.) plus five Republicans (Hruska, Fong, Thurmond, Cook, and Scott); but Sen. Scott restricted his approval to allowing the nomination to reach the Senate

floor without indicting how he would then vote. The negatives were Democrats Hart, Kennedy, Bayh, Burdick, and Tydings, and the Republican negative was Griffin.

25. *Senate Executive Report No. 91–12*, 91st Cong., 1st sess., Nov. 12, 1969, p. 12.

26. Ibid., 14.

27. Ibid., 24.

28. Ibid., 26.

29. Ibid., 31.

30. In the several-page discussion of this point (ibid., 32–38), Sen. Bayh cited no instance in which any judge was ever thought to be disqualified because of an interest in a supplier of a party; Judge Walsh and I had both said that there were no such cases. If there are any such cases, they remain still undiscovered.

31. Ibid., 46. Sen. Tydings was so impressed with Prof. Mellinkoff's letter that he largely adopted the statement as his own. When he came out against Haynsworth, after having originally promoted the appointment, he focused on the *Brunswick* matter, *Vend-a-Matic*, and the *Grace Lines* case. He then adopted essentially verbatim the language of the Mellinkoff letter. Sen. Mathias, also of Maryland, was troubled principally by the *Brunswick* case (Tydings to Robert A. Bolin, Nov. 12, 1969, Mathias to Robert A. Bolin, Nov. 17, 1969, Furman MSS).

VIII. Campaign and Debate

1. For illustration of some of the derision that Hancock received for his very sensible comment, see George F. Howe, *Chester A. Arthur* (New York: F. Ungar, 1935; rept. 1957), 123.

2. United Auto Workers broadside in Senate file.

3. The activities recounted in this chapter are drawn from the Walters MSS unless otherwise noted.

4. Haynsworth to Eastland, Oct. 7, 1969, Furman MSS.

5. Cook to Wolfstone, Oct. 15, 1969, Mollenhoff memorandum for files, Oct. 13, 1969, Department of Justice, FOIA.

6. 1971 interview. As will be developed, Haynsworth had a little more activity than this.

7. Wright to Rehnquist, Oct. 16, 1969, Wright collection.

8. Department of Justice, FOIA.

9. *Columbia Record*, Dec. 10, 1969.

10. *Columbia State*, Nov. 5, 1969.

11. *Columbia Record*, Nov. 10, 1969, expanded in *Columbia State*, Nov. 11, 1969.

12. *Time*, Nov. 14, 1969, 27.

13. AP Report, *Columbia Record*, Nov. 15, 1969.

14. Nov. 17, 1969, *Cong. Rec.*, 91st Cong., 1st sess., 34426.

15. Ibid., 34570.

16. Ibid., 34022.

17. Ibid., 34850.

18. The *Greenville News*, Oct. 18, 1969, 1, noted that $68,545 had been contributed by nineteen unions to Bayh's campaign fund when he ran for reelection in 1968.

19. *Cong. Rec.*, 91st Cong., 1st sess., 1969, 34854.

20. Sen. Javits concluded: "But I do distinguish the 'conservative' or 'liberal' cast of a judge, on the one hand, from a judge who persists in error—persists after years and years and years, in the view that the old was right and the new is wrong, particularly on this critical civil rights question. I do not feel that within my conscience I can, by my vote, send to the Court that judge, with that kind of philosophy. He is sincere—I do not denigrate or in any way deprecate the judge—but precisely because his philosophy is sincere, and I believe it is, I have to vote 'no' on his confirmation" (ibid., 34856).

21. Ibid., 35149.

22. Ibid., 35173-74.

23. Ibid., 35393.

24. Ibid., 35394.

25. *New York Times*, Nov. 22, 1969, 1.

IX. Postmortems

1. *Washington Star*, Nov. 23, 1969, 1.

2. John MacKenzie, "Haynsworth Foes Widen Their Drive," *Washington Post*, Sept. 9, 1969.

3. A particularly good illustration is a letter from Judge Edwin M. Stanley, the presiding judge for the Middle District of North Carolina: "I speak the sentiments of every district judge in the Circuit when I beg you to continue your work on the Court of Appeals, and to give no consideration whatever to rumors appearing in some press releases that you might consider resigning" (Stanley to Haynsworth, Nov. 21, 1969, Furman MSS).

4. Department of Justice, FOIA.

5. Walters MSS.

6. The telegram to the attorney general from sixteen past presidents of the ABA was sent on Oct. 23. William Gossett of Michigan declined to sign. Walters stressed to Mollenhoff, both on the phone and in a note, that the publicity should be handled without pointing at Gossett (ibid.).

7. Powell to William P. Dickson, Jr., of Norfolk, whom he left in charge of pro-Haynsworth affairs in Virginia for the period of his absence in Europe (ibid.).

8. *H.*, 128.

9. 1971 interview. Harry Haynsworth also participated in the interview.

10. Haynsworth to Eastland, Oct. 24, 1969, Furman MSS.

11. Ibid.

12. Haynsworth to Walters, Nov. 3, 1969, Walters MSS.

13. 1971 interview.

14. Mitchell interview, Washington, D.C., May 20, 1987.

15. *U.S. News and World Report*, Dec. 1, 1969, 88.

16. *Greenville News*, Nov. 22, 1969.

17. These passages are from a mass of letters in the Furman MSS written in the last few days of Nov. 1969.

18. Porter to Haynsworth, Nov. 25, 1969, ibid.

19. Black to Haynsworth, Nov. 21, 1969, Haynsworth to Black, Dec. 9, 1969, ibid. Other public figures sent telegrams of regret; two strong messages came from Sen. Robert Dole of Kansas and Sen. Barry Goldwater of Arizona. Attorney General Mitchell thought Haynsworth "very much of a man" for staying on the circuit (Mitchell interview, Washington, D.C., May 20, 1987).

20. Haynsworth to Graham, Nov. 26, 1969, Furman MSS.

21. Tower to Haynsworth, Dec. 1, 1969, Thurmond to Haynsworth, Dec. 2, 1969, ibid.

22. Haynsworth to Rehnquist, Dec. 2, 1969, ibid.

23. Powell to Haynsworth, Dec. 15, 1969, ibid.

24. 1971 interview.

25. Black to Haynsworth, Dec. 11, 1969, Furman MSS.

26. Rehnquist to Haynsworth, Nov. 21, 1969, Powell to President Nixon and Haynsworth, Nov. 22, 1969, Blackmun to Haynsworth, Nov. 25, 1969, ibid.

X. At Last an End: Carswell and Blackmun

1. Mitchell interview, Washington, D.C., May 20, 1987.

2. The biographical information on Carswell is taken largely from *Time*, Feb. 2, Feb. 9, 1970, 11; Judge Carswell's own sketch in the hearings on his confirmation, Senate Committee on the Judiciary, *Hearings on the Nomination of George Harrold Carswell to the United States Supreme Court*, 91st Cong., 2d sess., 1970, 10–11 (hereafter *H.*); and a comprehensive article in the *Washington Post*, Jan. 27, 1970, C1. I am indebted to my partner Alexandra M. Shafer for organization of much Carswell material.

3. Justice Hugo L. Black, conversation with author, Feb. 1970.

4. *Newsweek*, Feb. 9, 1970, 23.

5. *New York Times*, Jan. 20, 1970, p. 20, col. 3.

6. *Time*, Feb. 2, 1970, 8.

7. *New York Times*, Jan. 22, 1970, p. 1, col. 2.

8. *Time*, Feb. 2, 1970, 8; see also Richard Harris, *Decision* (New York: E. P. Dutton & Co., 1971), 16.

9. *H.*, 10–11.

10. Editorial, *Washington Post*, Jan. 21, 1970; *New York Times*, Jan. 21, 1970.

11. 411 F.2d 1 (5th Cir. 1969), petition for rehearing denied Oct. 13, 1969. The second rehearing, with Carswell participating, was denied at 416 F.2d 1257.

12. *Phillips v. Martin Marietta Corporation*, 400 U.S. 542, 91 S. Ct. 496, 27 L. Ed. 2d 613 (1971).

13. *New York Times*, Jan. 20, 1970.

14. *Washington Post*, Jan. 23, 1970.

15. The civil rights leadership conference had opposed Carswell for a circuit court position on the grounds that he had "been more hostile to civil rights cases than any other federal judge in Florida." Nonetheless, he was summarily confirmed. Rauh believed that the administration's choice of Carswell, the only man whom the leadership conference had ever opposed for the federal bench, was deliberately made in order to pick a fight with the leadership conference for the purpose of beating it in hand-to-hand combat (Harris, 29).

16. *Washington Post*, Jan. 27, 1970, A-1. The particular clipping used here is from Department of Justice FOIA files; handwritten on it, over the initial H. (Hoover?), is the line, "How did we miss this in our investigation of Carswell?"

17. *H.*, 12, 13.

18. Harris, 37.

19. Fred Graham, *New York Times*, Jan. 25, 1970.

20. *H.*, 6.

21. Harris, 45.

22. *H.*, 68.

23. Harris, 38.

24. *H.*, 113–32.

25. *H.*, 136.

26. *H.*, 224.

27. *H.*, 227.

28. *H.*, 239, 242, 247. It was quickly seen that those who opposed Haynsworth won a battle and lost a war when they got Carswell; see William S. White in the *Nashville Tennessean*, Jan. 25, 1970. Fred Graham also concluded that those who had opposed Carswell would have been better off if they had taken Haynsworth (*New York Times*, Jan. 25, 1970).

29. The procedures by which this result was achieved are well and dramatically described by Harris, 68–71.

30. *Washington Post*, Feb. 18, 1970.

31. Harris, 91, 92.

32. Ibid., 106. At that time, I was asked to join the Rosenman statement. Before doing so, I read the Carswell opinions comprehensively and concluded that Carswell was, indeed, an incompetent; I therefore joined in the statement. I was in touch with the then resigned justice Fortas at this time and on March 16, 1970, wrote him of this signature: "I have a comfortably egocentric sense of self satisfaction in this sequence—Haynsworth was not disqualified, and Carswell's not any good."

33. Any good trial judge should be reversed from time to time or he is too timid a judge, but Carswell was "more reversed than revered" (*Time*, Feb. 2, 1970, 81). For a report of the Columbia study, see ibid., Mar. 2, 1970, 15.

34. Harris, 124.

35. Ibid., 104.

36. Ibid., 110.

37. Former attorney general Mitchell regarded the Hruska statement as the coup de grace for Carswell. "If you knew Roman Hruska, you could expect something like that. He certainly took care of it in great style; but what he said just popped out" (Mitchell interview, Washington, D.C., May 20, 1987).

38. *Baltimore Sun*, Mar. 27, 1970.

39. Harris, 141–44.

40. *New York Times*, Mar. 28, 1970.

41. *Cong. Rec.*, 91st Cong., 2d sess., 1970, S.4945.

42. In Harris's view (170), while this memorandum revealed clearly that Carswell had deceived the Senate, it was of relatively little importance because most of the senators by then were committed one way or another. I do not share this view and believe that the falsehoods made the difference.

43. *Washington Evening Star*, Apr. 3, 1970. On Apr. 3 the district judges of the fifth circuit, led by Bryan Simpson, a circuit judge of Jacksonville, Florida, telegraphed the president endorsing the nomination. There were fifty-four names on the list.

44. Sen. Tydings had put the Horsky-Ramsey memorandum into the record with his own comments (*Cong. Rec.*, 91st Cong., 2d sess, 1970, 10167-71).

45. Ibid., 8068-69.

46. Ibid., 8805, 9263.

47. Ibid., 8078.

48. Ibid., 8381-83, 8715.

49. Ibid., 8703, 8721-23.

50. Ibid., 9283, 9315.

51. *Washington Post*, Apr. 7, 1970, A-1.

52. Harris, 180.

53. *Washington Evening Star*, Apr. 8, 1970, 1.

54. Harris, 113.

55. Ibid., 166.

56. *Washington Post*, Apr. 14, 1970, A-1.

57. Anderson, "Washington Merry Go Round," *Courier Express*, Apr. 18, 1970.

58. This, of course, did not happen.

59. Mitchell interview, Washington, D.C., May 20, 1987.

60. Senate Committee on the Judiciary, *Hearing on the Nomination of Harry A. Blackmun to the United States Supreme Court*, 91st Cong., 2d sess., 1970, 40 (hereafter *H.*).

61. *H.*, 38.

62. *H.*, 3.

63. *H.*, 41.

64. *H.*, 17.

65. *H.,* 11.

66. *Smith v. Board of Education,* 365 F.2d 770 (8th Cir. 1966); *Yarborough v. Hulbert–West Memphis School District,* 380 F.2d 962 (8th Cir. 1967).

67. *Jones v. Alfred H. Mayer Co., Meyer,* 379 F.2d 33 (8th Cir. 1967); *reversed* 392 U.S. 409 (1968).

68. *H.,* 13.

69. *Maxwell v. Bishop,* 398 F.2d 138 (8th Cir. 1968), *reversed* 398 U.S. 262 (1970). In 1987 as a justice of the Supreme Court, Blackmun wrote the major dissent on a case involving much more sophisticated statistical data in which, in light of the "statistical evidence," he concluded that "there exists in the Georgia capital-sentencing scheme a risk of racially biased discrimination that is so acute that it violates the Eighth Amendment" (*McClesky v. Kemp,* 107 S. Ct. 1756, 1794 [1987]).

70. *Jackson v. Bishop,* 404 F.2d 571 (1968).

71. *H.,* 35.

72. For example, *Mitchell v. Goodyear Tire & Rubber Co.,* 278 F.2d 562 (8th Cir. 1960), gives an employee more on a wage-hour case than the trial court allowed him; and *N.L.R.B. v. International Int. Union of Optg. Eng.,* 279 F.2d 951 (8th Cir. 1960) is more favorable to the union than was the Labor Board.

73. For illustration, in *N.L.R.B. v. Everqist,* 334 F.2d 312 (8th Cir. 1964), a majority of which Blackmun was one upheld the discharge of four union drivers who refused to cross the picket line of another union. This was a hard-fought issue with the Labor Board dividing three to two, and the circuit majority held that since there did not appear to be any antiunion animus, the discharges could stand. A dissenting judge felt that the drivers were entitled to their jobs back if they had not been already failed before they applied.

74. *H.,* 60.

75. *H.,* 63.

76. *Senate Executive Report,* 91st Cong., 2d sess., 1970, 91–18.

77. *Cong. Rec.,* 91st Cong., 2d sess., 1970, 14857-58, 15105-6.

78. Ibid., 15111.

79. Ibid., 15111.

80. Ibid., 15112.

81. Ibid., 15112-13, passim.

82. Ibid., 15117.

83. Ibid., 15684.

84. Ibid., 15688.

XI. Aftermath and Appraisal

1. *New York Times Magazine,* Aug. 1, 1971, 56.

2. Haynsworth to Mitchell, Nov. 26, 1969, Furman MSS.

3. Haynsworth to Nixon, Nov. 25, 1969, ibid. Gerald R. Ford, then the mi-

nority leader of the Republicans in the House of Representatives, told Haynsworth how much he admired the judge (Ford to Haynsworth, Nov. 28, 1969, ibid.).

4. Haynsworth to Nixon, Nov. 28, 1969, ibid.

5. *Chicago Tribune*, Dec. 5, 1969.

6. *Boston Herald Traveler*, Dec. 4, 1969.

7. Haynsworth to Bill Monroe, Dec. 8, 1969, Furman MSS.

8. *New York Times*, Oct. 18, 1971.

9. 1971 interview.

10. Furman MSS.

11. Powell to Haynsworth, Apr. 14, 1979, ibid.

12. 1971 interview.

13. *New York Times*, Apr. 21, 1970, 28; see also *Washington Post*, Apr. 21, 1970.

14. *New York Times*, July 13, 1970, 38, and Sept. 10, 1970, 38.

15. Ibid., June 27, 1976, 16, July 1, 1976, 14, and Oct. 2, 1976, 8.

16. John P. Frank, "The Burger Court: The First Ten Years," 43 *Law and Contemporary Problems* 107 (1980).

17. John P. Frank, a review of *The Brethren*, by Bob Woodward and Scott Armstrong, "The Supreme Court: The Muckrakers Return," 66 *American Bar Association Journal* 162 (1979).

18. There are minor differences not relevant to the main account being given here.

19. Chief Justice Traynor was at the height of his preeminent reputation as the leading state judge of the country. I remember the warmth and excitement in every senatorial and congressional office which Judge Traynor and I visited as the youthful staff members of congressmen and senators poured out of their own offices to greet the great judge.

20. For details, see Frank, 1972 *Utah L. Rev.* 377. Sen. Quentin Burdick of North Dakota, Rep. Robert Kastenmeier of Wisconsin, and the then Rep. William Cohen, now a senator from Maine, were particularly helpful in passing the new law.

21. Mitchell interview, Washington, D.C., May 20, 1987.

22. *New York Times*, July 12, 1987, 1.

Index